SEA-GIRT CITADEL

Surgeon Goes to War in Shetland

by

Daniel Lamont

To the late Sir John Fraser, K.C.V.O., M.C., F.R.C.S., Emeritus Professor of Clinical Surgery and Principal of Edinburgh University.

THE SHETLAND TIMES LTD.

1973

PREFACE

Possibly the sole merit of this book is the pleasure that it has afforded its perpetrator by the writing of it, in the loud, raucous watches of the night. That, be it said, is in no way to imply that, given the opportunity, he would gladly elect to relive some of the incidents disclosed. Far from it; the suffering in an armchair before the television screen has nowadays much more of an appeal.

There may be some who think that flippancy, degradation and worse, are ill-matched yoke-mates. But words were given us for more purposes than one and I am not at all sure but that the most important is the hiding of our thoughts.

And besides, an approach with lugubriousness of mien does not contribute a whit of gladness to the mental state of any patient when the surgeon's bleeding bowl is brought close to his side; nor do salt-laden tears have much of curative value if they be splashed over the expectant brim.

What the surgeon really feels deep, deep down is, moreover, entirely his affair and his alone; so, in that context, I am hopeful that, if even only now and then, a tiny gleam of more than sub-human sympathy may peep through the gore-drenched crypts of these pages.

"Causerie" has been used to describe my ramblings; it could be that "chaos" were a better term, for something of a game of leap-frog has been played with the sequence of events in chronological occurrence. To the author, all the same, there is an associated and rational connection but there again, this sensibility may be his and his alone.

CONTENTS

Illustrations between pages 48 - 49.

CHAPTER I

Brought up by godly parents I passed my days of childhood and adolescence in a comparatively sheltered regimen within the aura of the Scottish manse.

True, in the carefree days of school, the more vigorous forms of sport were never at all neglected but these early formative years were destined to be rudely displaced by the combative orgy of war.

To these three factors, godliness, sport and war, I know now, in maturity, that my continued survival is attributable, for they taught me how to care for my body and to defend myself when need arose, provided, of course, that a particular bullet with my name on it did not silence me first!

Since these early foundations were established, my lot in life seems to have been cast amidst a turmoil of violence and trauma; in the wiser days as healer of those who have suffered pain as have I.

I regret none of it; I have learned to know men and to much lesser extent, women. I have found from time to time solace and stimulation in the glorious company of the erudite, the brave, the cultured, but my greatest joy has ever been the contact with the common folk. I admire and think that I understand the clever business executive of high integrity. I respect the members of the learned professions, but had I to choose again I believe I should repeat my first offence and run away once more from the danger of becoming a fashionable surgeon. That fate, I would stress, was perilous for me as an individual only and in no way would I belittle my successful professional colleagues: I rejoice in their ascendancy. It is simply that I acknowledge freely that I never was endowed with the imaginative genius of a Learmonth, the finely analytical mind of Dan Cappell, John Young and other year-mates who reached professorial eminence.

I have found my *métier* in the succouring of the men from whose ranks come the craftsmen, the carpenters, the fishermen, the engine-drivers and others of the vast cohort we know as the working classes — admittedly a spurious term of segregation but it will serve, I trust, to convey what I intend.

The Kaiser's war instilled in my undeveloped mind an intense longing to be in it, not, I am sure, because I wanted "to do my bit" but because most of my intimate friends, who were invariably my seniors by a year or so, were burgeoning daily into martial resplendancy and my ardent boyish need was to be upsides with them.

The first essay in this direction was anything but propitious. It all began with a yachting regatta on that sailing paradise, the beautiful, fluky Firth of Clyde, at a place, Tigh - na - Bruaich, approached away westward through the enchanting narrows of the Kyles of Bute.

Mr Peter Dunlop, scion of a famous Scottish shipping family and son of Sir Thomas Dunlop, Bart., Lord Provost of Glasgow, was at that time the target of profound hero-worship by me. Numbered amongst the fleet of Dunlop-owned craft Peter had *Terrier,* a fast half-decked motor boat, built of double-skinned diagonal planking.

He was also owner of *Kitten,* a not-so-fast open rowing boat powered by an outboard Evinrude engine.

During the closing days of 1914's racing, the latter ship was entrusted to my steersmanship for the Tigh-na-Bruaich regatta.

My one-man crew was feminine — my sister Vera; she, poor lass, was ordered forward right into the bows to act as ballast.

Thus nicely trimmed and full of high hopes, we weighed anchor at Innellan, where my family had a residence, and made to round Toward Point on our passage to the starting line.

About the Powder Buoy, abreast the Point, tide, wind and sea were all at variance and so contrived to throw up quite a considerable bit of a chop.

Luckless Vera did not much appreciate the sheets of spray coming inboard, but the steersman, with precocious sea-wise lore, told her calmly that it could not last long — he was merely punching into the rip to avoid the inconvenience of turning turtle.

Thus reassured she was misguided enough to put up her umbrella.

Immediate disaster was somehow circumvented — disaster from the elements that is; retribution was to overtake us presently from quite another quarter. At this moment, however, the wind, warming to its work of rebuke at this flagrant defiance, snatched away the absurdity, now turned inside out, from doting sister's agitated clutching and, with louder snorts than ever, spun our frail craft round and round.

This precise moment *had* to be chosen for the lovely and gracious S.Y. *Ariadne* to pass this way, a stately, disapproving witness of all our evolutions.

Sir Thomas, with his famous Master, Captain Mac, was on the bridge.

He was waiting for me at the slip-way when I had but made my landfall up the Kyles.

"I never thought I should live to see the day when an umbrella —an UMBRELLA — would be hoisted on a Dunlop-owned vessel, racing craft or dinghy!

"A tarry-fingered land lubber in the west Bay of Dunoon at the Fair Holidays might pass but . . . you . . . you . . . in a boat of mine . . . right under the eyes of my own crew . . . !"

He was even more elemental than the elements!

I thus went to the starting line with my nautical tail well and truly between my stern sheets. But, I thought, if I could, with the aid of my astronomical time-allowance, go on to win, the day might be saved to some extent.

It did not turn out that way, though. In the muster of fourteen roaring, tearing, spume-swept furies, I rounded the mark on the first leg, placed number thirteen of the line.

On the second and final leg I did not prove quite so successful.

Peter, who was winner, was to provide a great fount of solace. Embarked on *Terrier,* with *Kitten* in tow, we made for Innellan where he was our guest for the night. To me was entrusted the wheel of the sleek twenty-knot racer.

On arrival I beached my first command then turned to Vera whose aplomb was now fully restored; I suggested we have a really fast run on my recently acquired T.T. Matchless motor cycle, a rakish affair with down-swept handle-bars and canoe side-car.

She agreed with alacrity and hoisted herself into the streamlined, doorless appurtenance.

My own posture was remarkable. My chin narrowly missed impinging on the top of the petrol tank and my arms were splayed widely like a jockey's over Becher's Brook as I caressed the low-set grips; the speedometer, capable of recording eighty miles per hour, all but brushed my tousled forelock.

Our course was set again for Toward to the South'ard; it had to be for Northaway there awaited me yet another Nemesis — in the village. In this case it was our local constable who had thrice warned (for the last time on each occasion) that the roar from an unsilenced motor cycle engine was an offence against the law.

It is true that the village blacksmith, a friend of mine for whom I willingly and frequently acted as bellows-boy or even striker, had fashioned a most elegant and shiny black-enamelled cylinder of tin. Its mooring, however, to the long drag of the exhaust pipe, contrived by some quite recondite method in the smiddy, was just a little dubious. Hence, this evening's sortie was by way of being somewhat experimental.

A trial it certainly was to be, for sister Vera!

Nicely rounding the right-hand curve at The Priory — bodies well inclined over to counter centrifugal force — side-car wheel six inches off the ground — much dust and showing off! But with it all, blessed silence! Lovely, smooth click of tappets — nothing louder — as yet!

For the nice long piece of straight ahead I opened up the throttle to the full!

Forward leapt the goaded monster.

Bang! Shot the lovely, black-enamelled projected missile,, careering, whirling, bouncing right back to its point of no return, three hundreds yards astern.

Simultaneously, with a sudden release of Thor's loudest reverberations, my Sleipnir darted forward with the rush of a meteorite for, alas, the sister-bearing canoe appurtenance had cut right adrift.

All I glimpsed, for the fraction of a second, was the side-car, stabilised on an even keel by transmitted speed, whirl with tremendous impetus in a contracting arc in the direction of the beautiful sun-kissed Firth of Clyde.

Loving Smile of Sister Kind was, for the moment entirely effaced but I could not just then be of much assistance! a speed wobble, fetching me perilously near the gates of Allan Park, where dwelt my friend Morton Weir, now Lord Inverforth, but then convulsed with mirth, was claiming all my resource and roadmanship.

In time, I picked an indignant but unscathed sister out of a mound of hay which mercifully had intercepted her parabolic flight to the sea.

The talk that night, around our drawing room, was all of war and what that meant. My elder brother, Ernest, was knowledgeable in respect of the South African campaign but Peter it was who knew what submarine attack could mean. He spoke of counter measures too, patrols at sea and what Clyde yachtsmen might be called upon to do.

I sat enthralled until parental mandate signalled that the time for retiral was upon me.

Rising to bid goodnight, my aching heart was soon to receive the balm for which it craved after the still-smarting *Ariadne* encounter. And the tribute came from no less a one than my hero, dear beloved Peter.

There were two other visitors; one was my Uncle Dan, before long to be in action in the Senior Chaplain's Department with the First Battalion of the King's Own Scottish Borderers and some thirteen years later to be the Very Reverend Moderator to the General Assembly of the Church of Scotland whilst he was Professor of

Christian Ethics and Practical Theology in the University of Edinburgh.

The other was "Dynamite Dan," or more formally, Mr Daniel Fleming. The soubriquet was his by virtue of his association as director with an explosive firm, allied to Nobel.

"Dynamite Dan," later to become a very good friend, was then the owner of a black ten-ton cutter *Violet*, rather an unseaworthy and leaky old tub, in my fastidious judgment.

He was speaking of plans for the morrow as I prepared to leave the room.

"I suppose I can count on you as crew, Danny?" He addressed me.

With all my ambitions for the following day focused on *Terrier* and the propinquity of Peter, I answered in the negative.

There was momentary silence in the room as I passed through the doorway but I caught "Dynamite Dan's" next words:

"I suppose the young beggar's got the wind up."

Impulsively I made to return and refute such a dastardly calumny. Thus I caught Peter's instant rejoinder and my uncle's acquiescence.

"Don't you believe that, Dan; young Danny's got more spunk than the two of us put together. My father says that I could not do better than sign him on as snotty if we're called on to mobilise and I completely agree."

Unashamedly I was now frankly eavesdropping as the eminent third Dan spoke:

"Indeed, Mr Dunlop, I do believe that what you say is right. What would Duncan and Christina have to say about it?"

I could not see through the partially closed door but as my parents returned no word I could picture my father's wise, kind eyes, twinkling merrily and my mother's lovely features wreathed in smiles.

Thus ended for me the day of my very first combined land and sea operation; had I, at that time, been familiar with a cryptic signal I came in after years to recognise often and to learn of all the travail, grief and horror that must inevitably precede its display, I should have made the hoist right then: "mission successfully accomplished."

The sequel to it all occurred when, with war now under way, Peter appeared devastatingly in our town house "Inveryne." He was thus early Lieutenant Dunlop, Coastal Motor Boat Patrol, Auxiliary Naval Service and *Terrier* was his first command wearing its ensign.

Quite obviously, in the natural order of things, I must be his

Chief of Staff or at least as near to that exalted appointment as my tender years would permit.

Peter was willing, I was willing but, unhappily, the two of us were in a minority of precisely that number.

I was interviewed by Commodore the Duke of Montrose, K.T., in an office above the outfitting emporium, Paisley's, in Glasgow.

Before mounting to the Presence, I had dallied for the half hour which was the measure of my too-early optimistic arrival, to gloat over the assorted display of maritime attire in the huge establishment: I had indeed specifically ear-marked the particular garb I should have and was concerned only in the matter of size in my assuredness of a successful interview; there was no consideration given to the possibility of rejection.

"Does your father know you're here?" was all I was asked.

Like someone else of somewhat more illustrious name, I could not tell a lie.

"Come back when you have his permission — in writing." Thus did His Grace pipe me over the side.

Disillusioned, disconsolate and demoralised I debouched into the Broomielaw, in my eyes, a disgusting looking place.

CHAPTER II

My next bid was for a Sam Browne belt. I filled up all the papers — Higher Leaving Certificate from school, "Cert. 'A'" from the Cadet Corps, testimonial of superb character from Sir William Bilsland who was seeing me for the first time in his life when he handed it to me in the City Chambers: "That's all right, my boy, I know your mother and father very well."

In due course, along with seven other aspirants of twice my stature, I was interviewed in the Headquarters of Glasgow University's Senior O.T.C. by two red-tabbed ferocities and a nincompoop of a captain who laughed on my entry.

They barely read my painstakingly concocted application for temporary Commissioned Rank in His Majesty's Imperial Forces ("preferably Highland Regiment: willing to serve overseas. Unmarried").

"Come back in two years' time — if it's not all over by then;" was all I got in place of "To our Trusty and Well-beloved, Greeting. We, reposing especial Trust and Confidence in your Loyalty, Courage and Good Conduct . . . . " for which my heart was yearning.

Many, that black morning, were called but few were chosen. Of the eight candidates, only one made the grade, but then he was the sole Public School applicant and these were early days yet!

Six of us rejects, who were all friends, held earnest colloquy; our decision was unanimous. Buckling on our halberds the posse marched on Argyle Street, the objective to be stormed — the Recruiting Office where was displayed irrefutable graphic evidence that Kitchener wanted us. I was pleased to observe that he particularly desired me, for every time I looked his poised fingers pointed right in my direction.

Our intention had been to join up in the Argyll and Sutherland Highlanders; we liked the kilt and we liked the green rosettes the officers sported on it.

Entering the bare-board foyer, with its walls festooned by posters, we were horrified to see behind the G.S. trestle-table, a particular *bête-noire* of ours, a fellow under-graduate, vulgarly flaunting a very new single pip on his braided sleeve. He was staring superciliously above an over-polished Sam Browne belt.

"Great jumping Jehosophat!" ejaculated our "Cupid" (in later

7

life, Doctor John MacBride, M.D., of Harley Street). "Just suppose
we were to get *that* for a Platoon Commander!"

The hazard was much too great to risk; with one accord,
smartly and in unison, toe of the right foot to heel of the left, about
we turned and changed direction right. Now it was "Objective,
secondary — assault unsuccessful, in event of" and we made for
Bath Street where the mustachioed and ubiquitous Kitchener still
insisted that he needed our services.

The recruiting sergeant here was a refreshing change from
Second Lieutenant Self-Satisfaction at Argyle Street and he seemed
to like the look of us; callers, obviously, were not very numerous

"Before your attestation, what is it your fancy to join?" he
asked.

I was first to speak: "Scottish Horse." I startled the unsuspect-
ing troop-to-be beside me.

"Can any of you ride?"

"Of course." Again I spoke for all although "Cupid" confided
in a nervous whisper that he didn't know the sharp end from the
blunt.

"I'll show you; I can tell them both;" I adjured him.

"But will it be safe?" he then wanted to know.

By this time the green-sashed sergeant, who had momentarily
left us, returned with an officer wearing gorgets of similar hue.

"Hello, Arthur"; I piped up and the mountebank Arthur
Douglas, of our own year, deigned to answer; "Hello, Dan; you there?"

Then the likeable villain told us that the Scottish Brigade
of Yeomanry was a pretty choosy outfit. What had any of us of
special merit to recommend his acceptance within the stables of
its select squadrons?

I could not very well advance my one valid reason that I
liked the nice array of brass buttons on the sleeve and the tasty
line in diced bonnets of the famous Scottish Horse.

I compromised with the statement which was one-sixth true;
"We all like horses."

That got by. The sergeant took our particulars; we took the
oath but did not get any shilling.

Second Lieutenant Arthur Douglas gave us our orders; "Report
to St. Mary's Hall, Lanark, tomorrow before five o'clock."

Arthur had only been in uniform about ten minutes so he
couldn't be blamed for failing to know the military usage by which
post-meridian time may be distinguished from ante-meridian with
considerable exactitude. Anyway, Arthur wouldn't have been able
to count up to twelve accurately, let alone juggle with innumerable
zeros. All the same, as we were to agree later, he *should* have been
capable of directing us to the Scottish Horse in Perthshire and not

to the Lanarkshire Yeomanry at St. Mary's Hall.

Not knowing this at the time as we filed out of Bath Street I was in a reverie for another reason. It's a funny thing, I was musing, one could not tell a lie directly to the representatives of the War Office, but a recruiting sergeant seemed to be different for I had aged two years, it was recorded, from the moment I had filled in the attestation form.

From these haphazard beginnings began the long, painful and circuitous route that led to the Second Battle of Ypres, from Steenstate to Langemarck; to the first chlorine gas and the improvised mask of home-knitted socks, soaked in the only home-produced fluid available to surprised Tommies; Loos, Vimy Ridge — out on rest at Bethune (cheery Mademoiselle that in the chemist's shop!) Hazebruick Railhead and the earning of a first wound stripe when honoured by individual attention from a roving Taube.

None the less one treasured through it all a sense of fine comradeship but many, many friends were lost.

Then there was the interminable mud-existence of the First Battle of the Somme ("You are fighting to relieve pressure on Verdun!") Delville Wood! Fight for your life against the Hun, fight him tooth and nail but most of all fight like the devil to save yourself from being another of these dead Jocks — stuck in the swamp and drowned or just picked off; 20,000 officers and 480,000 men, all to fester away!

Fight the Hun! Remember your training, "The Spirit of the Bayonet" — take that, you bastard (turn the blade) out — quick — heave a Mill's bomb — got the swine!

On further — the spirit of the bayonet — kick him even if he's dead! Take prisoners? Ye Gods, who is there to take the b....s back? No fear! Shoot them — good — come on, Jocks, Blighty's not far away but first Kill! Kill! Kill! Hi you, Canada, lend a hand and boot this swine off my bayonet — I've got him through the spine and I'm jammed. Good! Kick him in the face — harder!

On to that next smashed-up duckboard; Oh, Gee, it's a lovely war! My holy goodness, what's that lying there? Right enough it's that sod of a captain from "Q" Squadron. Gee, shot right in the back too! His own chaps have done it after all, just as they said they would.

Come on, then, you Hun, come at me! You bloody fool, you've lost your head; you should have shot me — not tried to stick me when I've fallen: you can't lunge at me from up there in all this mire and not get it through the guts — put your butt across his skull for me, Jock — he's wriggling still. Gosh! Here's another of the brutes! At the throat and heart — point! On guard — up! Damn! Where's my bloody rifle got to now? Ah, well! Here's the end for young Danny. Come on, Fritz — you win: here's my boot, all the same — as hard as I can — right in your crutch — just for luck — you slimy, great big bastard!

*   *   *   *   *

Why, it's very dark and still out here on the water. This must be the Kyles of Bute and I've fallen asleep at the helm. But who are these two lying beside me? They're awful white and quiet: they must be deck hands, surely.

Let me look again — hang it, these are dead Huns and that's not water — it's mud; Oh, I begin to see: I've copped another packet — and a bad one too it is, I 'm sure. So this is death coming up! Right, then; I've already thought all this out and know I'll just sink away from sight: Mother and Vera and poor old Dad — they'll be broken-hearted but they'll know I tried to do my best.

"My heavenly Father, I beseech thee; forgive me all the sins I have committed. I asked for it, God, and I got it: now I am ready to come to thee."

*   *   *   *   *

Hello Padre! What's the big white marquee for? Where am I? In a C.C.S.? Oh, that's nice when you put your hand on my brow— thank you. Am I here to be de-loused?

Oh, Padre! Where are all my half-sections — MacCallum, Cameron, Bannatyne? They're all killed? They're dead? — Oh, Oh, I'm so sorry Padre, I can't help crying — like a kid, who's hurt himself — Oh, Banny, poor old Banny. Hello, Orderly; that needle for me? Don't you come near me, you bloody Hun! Take that — take that; you S....t! Oh, I'm sorry, old chap: I'm sorry, Padre — I'll be good, yes, good, good if you say so — kill the bastards — kill, ki' — ki' — ki' — .

Boulogne! Hello, Nurse! Why am I alone in this room with screens round me? What's that above my head — the red stuff in the bottle? Blood, you say? What's it there for? I'm glad it's not bloody mud, anyway! Oh, you would go for my mouth, would you? Take that then!

Oh, Nurse! I'm so sorry I've bitten clean through your thermometer: I thought it was some bloo — something else! I'll be good, Nurse, yes, if you say so — good, good — needle, needle again — nothing but steel: can't get away, can't get back — on, on, anywhere. Sleep, you fool, sleep . . . .

Ambulance — boat — fell off the stretcher waiting at the gangway: who's that giving someone a telling-off?

"You damned fools, bearers! I told you to have another man to watch him: the case is delirious — he might have killed himself. Go to sleep, Sonnie, no one's going to hurt you now."

"'Thank you, Doctor."

Folkestone — bombs — frightened. Train at last; Hello, Sister! Bottle of stout? Yes, rather — anything wet: I'm thirsty, oh, so thirsty. Parents? Yes, of course I have. What — I'll see them in London? Oh, good: they'll maybe bring me a present — my Saturday sixpence, perhaps. Wait a minute, though, Sister:; why London? I'm going home to the Clyde — I'll see the parents there: my mother was born in the Clyde Valley, you know — where the apple blossom grows, up near Lanark — maybe that's why fate shoved me into the Lanarkshire Yeomanry although we all thought it was Arthur Douglas, the mug, who botched it all. Our horses didn't remain long but never mind, we had a nice red stripe down our breeches and we kidded ourselves we were still Yeomanry by keeping our dismounted cavalry drill: wasn't much help when it came to being drafted in amongst the Jocks, though! (Remember to keep my boots round my neck in the ambulance, also my death-button and my ammo.)

Where are my pals, Sister? 'M' Squadron's Commander— Major Younger, "Iron Guts" we called him. Made us march twenty miles with full pack and then swim the Tay. Good old Major Younger — owns a brewery, so they say. (You're not forgetting my stout, I hope, Sister?)

Then there was Squadron Sergeant-Major Provan; where are you? You were good to me — put me up for a third stripe, I remember, and always stood up for me. You came from Lanarkshire too — Lesmahagow (I told you my mother was very beautiful? They called her the Belle of Lanark).

Ah, there you are, Sister, with my bottle of stout? Oh, you mean thing, it's that cursed needle again — and a blunt sod too. Ouch!

Where? Charing Cross and No. 3 General Hospital. Well, well — me for home and glory. Up the Lanarks!

I thought I was going to the Clyde Valley, Nurse? This is another damned operating theatre!

Ah, well, sleep, sleep, sleep: I'm going home to Inveryne — home will be nice — Clyde Valley, will your apple blossom ever come again?

CHAPTER III

"I've made mistakes, of course, but never the same one twice."

How often that smug claim has been voiced to me by men, estimated by the standards of some, to be successful in life.

For myself, I can record neither immunity from errors nor even this single performance in the committing of them. Throughout life my minor mistakes have been repeated over and over again, often with intervals of years between certainly, but in major misjudgments I generally have two goes before I can profit by the warning light when the third potential crisis of similar nature presents itself.

There is one particular precept it has taken me a lifetime to learn effectively: "Never interfere betwen a donna and her man." The police everywhere, be it Tangiers or Townhead, appreciate the value of this injunction and no Freudian apostle is needed to explain why the female spits and caterwauls when the amorous male pussy buries his teeth in her neck and pulverises her with passion. But let another Tom intervene! He will then have two ferocious enemies to face and the gentler sex is the worse of these.

The first experience of this sort befell me as a youth, callow in civilised sin but well versed in war, when I was supposed to be engaged in relaxation.

I was at the time quartered in St. John's Wood with "B" Reserve Brigade of the Royal Horse Artillery in the probationary stages of officer cadetship, with aspirations to commissioned rank in that most illustrious of corps. The thirteen-pounder gun drill at Lords, the stretch gallop wheeling left and right in Regent's Park, the tan of the riding school, the hazards of the rough-riders' course, the mathematical juggling with the slide-rule — none of these presented any real terrors to a pilgrim not long since a mere schoolboy. I had, by this time, assimilated a sufficiency of military lore to know how best to present whatever talents I did happen to possess or to invent them when non-existent.

What did cause dismay on many occasions was the recurring threat hurled at me of that ignominious fate "Returned to Unit." This stemmed from my apparent inability to comport myself with the very essence of punctilio demanded by the superlative standards set by the commanding officer, Lieut.-Col. Lord Alfred Browne.

Although I might spend hours squatting on my palliasse, furbishing arms and accoutrements, in all probability my illustrious cap-badge would be pronounced off the straight by the lynx-eyed section officer at 9 a.m. parade. Or again, there would be a smut on the virginal whiteness of my cap band and my plaited lanyard would be twisted. Always something, be it buttons, boots or breeches.

In the enjoyment of concentrated study and hard physical exercise all of this secret worry faded from mind but later, in my leisure moments, I brooded over it and persuaded myself into the conviction that there was some sort of hoodoo over me — plagued by Gremlins, your modern R.A.F. type would have it!

A source of great comfort to me at this time was the companionship of another medical student, a Liverpudlian named Felix Q. McKeown, later to be heavily decorated for outstanding bravery in the face of the enemy. We had first met, in mutual chagrin, "on the mat," before Lord Alfred. I forgot what was Felix Q's particular misdemeanour now but he was one of the blond, carefree, merry-eyed kind who much preferred to wear his service cap tilted right back on his occiput and his straying forelock was very apt to peep out in most un-R.H.A.-like manner. His tie, too, when we were resplendent in our "glad rags," was wont to migrate round his neck a bit. With unremitting regularity we paraded together on that horrid little square of carpet with an equally horrid Warrant Officer bawling at us all the time. And thus the bonds of friendship were fashioned in the common travail.

There came a day when the two of us set off for our first incursion into the West End. Truth to tell I had never been at liberty in London before; my transit through it had hitherto always been in troop trains or ambulance wagons and beyond the Strand and Piccadilly I knew the names of no streets. On this pleasure jaunt we did contrive to find our way to Whitehall but our passing of Horse Guards Parade was anything but auspicious.

We were, within our individual competences, correctly dressed — white cap-band; black, highly polished G-S field boots; burnished spurs; gleaming white belt with that abomination, a sabre in its metal scabbard, suspended therefrom. As if it weren't enough to be obliged to salute — timing exactly as in the drill book too! — every officer encountered without having to control that confounded toothpick which clanked waywardly on the pavement at the merest hint of relaxation! The metropolis was literally teeming with gold braid and pips and for an officer cadet to ignore one carried the very live risk of being stopped and questioned, as likely as not to be further reprimanded for failure to stand properly at attention during the routine harangue, and even of being reported to Lord Alfred —

and everything which that connoted in "Returned to Unit!"

Felix Q and I knew all about it before long! It happened plumb in front of the Life Guards sentries and later my feeling was that the old dug-out who did it chose the particular scene merely for effect and to boost his ego.

We had been progressing reasonably smartly and efficiently (we thought!) towards an undefined objective, eyes left, eyes right, trying to catch a glimpse of any of the magical sights of London but wary as cats all the time not to miss a pip. We made special endeavour as we came up to the sentries. "The Pride of the British Army, the Right of the Line," we knew ourselves to be — or going to be if we evaded R.T.U.! — and Life Guards had nothing on us!

In all this fierce concentration of effort we completely failed to see Red Tabs. "Looked exactly like a nanny-goat," Felix Q epitom-ised later but I was too hypnotised to see anything but red.

"What do you call yourselves?" he barked; "Music Hall turn or a half-section of bog-spavined loafers?"

"Beg pardon, Sir; we didn't see you;" came out from the readier witted Felix Q. in heavy but honeyed Lancashire accents.

"Wheel round — walk march twenty paces; wheel again and approach me properly. Action, both of you — at once!"

Now, this manoeuvre, even to the elementary military student, presents no problem at all but make the venue a Whitehall crowded with fascinated onlookers, add to the milieu a traffic jam with taxis and buses affording a grandstand view, quite free, and over-shadowing all project two robots, immobile, but for their crinkling eyes, as the pillars of the temple of Boaz! Now throw in the complicated clutch-ings and legerdemain needed to manipulate two metal scabbards (and all that in the correct timing, according to the book, too) and maybe you'll see what I mean! Anyway, the two of us forgot to salute before we set off on our circus act which omission immediately provoked further caustic comment but, at least, we were not without our sympathisers; two enormous Aussies winked at us and slouched past Red Tabs, their hands well buried in their pockets. One of them happened to be familiar. I recognised George Howell at once, even had I not glimpsed the brand new maroon-coloured ribbon, with miniature cross, in front of his Military Medal.

Felix Q and I finished our sight-seeing by bus.

Later, as dusk was falling we ventured into Lyons' Corner House and there, after careful perusal of the tariff, we satisfied our ravenous appetites. I was somewhat better off financially than my companion as I had attained to the exalted rank of Troop Corporal (acting Sergeant) whilst with the Yeomanry Brigade and I was still paid the extra two shillings the rank carried. On the strength of my superior capitalistic state Felix Q elected to devour an extra fourpenny pie.

By the time we came out darkness was sufficiently advanced for us very knowledgeable students of King's Regulations to know that the saluting need no longer worry us. With this realisation came a general easing off in the rigidity of our deportment and we transgressed so far as to loiter around the corner of Haymarket and Piccadilly, just to watch the people.

That was my undoing.

In the endless stream of service strollers there presently came heaving into view the familiar diced bonnet of the Lovat Scouts. I recognised the wearer; both having qualified as marksmen we had at one time been selected for special Field Reconnaissance duties. Nowadays they call them Commandos: they are glamorised — we were anything but and, as it happened, most of the lot were killed or captured on Gallipoli peninsula.

I soon also recognised the aptness of the word "heaving" as my friend drew near; what I did not, at the moment, appreciate was the status of the brace of *filles de joie* tailing on behind him. Of course, at this stage of my career I did know something of the bees, the birds and little lady bow-wows, but really, apart from my recent army service, mine had been a sheltered scholastic existence, centred mainly around the sports ground and the charms of the boudoir had never been included.

I hailed my erstwhile Lovat buddy with enthusiasm and he responded with true Gaelic if somewhat bibulous sentiment.

Felix Q stood rather aloof; he had a complex about Assistant Provost Marshals, even in the dark. Consequently, for a while the animation was confined to us Scotsmen until one of the V-necked ladies, who had likewise heaved-to, slipped a hand through my sabre-less arm and mouthed her piece; "What about you coming along with me, Duckie? I know where to go."

The deliberate pressure of her bosom against me was nauseatingly embarrassing and I knew that I was blushing.

But up spoke my Scout; "Man, Dan; that's a fine notion. The leave train's no' till ten an' we can get a taxi; I'll pay."

I was tongue-tied; I had never been in a situation such as this but chivalry demanded that I refrained from telling her too pointedly she was on a loser.

Felix Q, however, for the moment suffered from no such inhibition. I think really he was nervous for the remark he made was quite unlike himself, although its implication was strictly according to the book, as inculcated into every one of us soldiers.

"Clap, clap! Here comes the bride!"

The result was startling and I, more than anyone, was to

know it. The second lady, a sylph-like creature who had not so far done more than show her teeth, hit me hard on the nose with the back of her hand. Inside my cranium somewhere I sensed a click and I was acutely aware of a very sore pain. Worse than anything a warm trickle was soon to caution me that disaster was imminent for my immaculate accoutrements if I didn't bring a handkerchief into use with all dispatch. In a panic I let go sabre, scabbard and all to clatter about my feet whilst I strove to staunch the flow. The particular corner where we stood was anything but private and a halt was made by everyone within range of us, Felix Q and I the unenviable cynosure of all eyes for the second time on this memorable day.

"You've broken his nose;" informed my fellow medical whose clinical studies had been really quite supererogatary to arrive at the diagnosis.

"Gosh, it's all squint;" marvelled the Scout and I wasn't any more comforted. With resentment in my soul I viewed the crowd and in ironical acceptance of the inevitable muttered the inspiring words of the Royal Regiment's motto: *"Obique quo Fas et Gloria ducunt;"* the spectre of R.T.U. was very close just then!

The Sylph was still showing a hankering after her Scout but he announced clearly he had no inclination to desert us, although I was fervently wishing he would. My inamorata, muttering imprecations, just melted away and the limpet one, also abusive, then followed her. I judged we had better move too and as we had already that day gazed on the façade of St. George's Hospital I intimated that I wanted to go there.

"Nae need for that;" says Jock; "You'll be all right till the morn when ye can report sick."

Handkerchief to face with one hand and the cursed scabbard re-levitated in the other I stared at him witheringly. But, of course, it was futile to try and explain to him that I should require to present an adequate explanation for my plight; the truth would be disastrous and no circumstantial equivocation would avail with Lord Alfred's hierarchy.

Now, from Piccadilly to St. George's is no great distance but in the circumstances of that night it could have been a London to Brighton walk for me. Jock's largesse in the matter of a taxi could not extend to such a silly mission as the present — he being a ghillie from Rosshire — and I recoiled from the thought of public transport.

Ultimately we entered the forecourt and I had my first intro-dution to a Casualty Department; everybody was really very pleasant including the white-coated Registrar, a title which was quite unknown to me then and I wondered if he held some clerical post until he took a good gander all around and inside my injured member. Then he devastated me with his pronouncement: "You've dislocated your nasal bones but don't worry, there's an E.N.T. list tomorrow morning and one of the Honoraries will straighten it out for you — under a general anaesthetic, of course."

"Can't I have it done now?" I beseeched him.

"Not poss., old thing; the E.N.T. Surgeon will tap it back into position with a hammer and then we'll X-Ray it. It ought to be all right."

"Can't *you* do that; here and now?"

He shook his head: "Beastly sorry and all that but it would mean opening up the Theatre just for one simple little thing that can well wait and, anyway, you'd never be back for Lights Out tonight as you'd need time to recover from the anaesthetic."

Simple little thing that can well wait! Easy to see that he knew nothing about Lord Alfred, Captain Sponson, Battery-Sergeant-Major Greenaway or that putrid little square of carpet in the first named's Orderly Room!

"Look here, Doctor;" I begged of him; "You biff it back, never mind the anaesthetic. I've complete faith in you; it will be fine. I must be back in St. John's Wood by ten tonight and I can't possibly report sick tomorrow. Please help me out! It means my very commission to me."

"It would hurt like blazes," he told me.

"No it wouldn't; it's all numb now and anyway it hurt like blazes when I got it and it can't be any worse going back."

I don't quite know what the line of reasoning was but he finally yielded to my pleading.

It wasn't at all pleasant, I admit: but Felix Q stood by to hold my hand and the Fidus Achates even went the length of paying the fares in the Tube that got us back to barracks just in time for Roll Call.

Naturally, the swelling and discoloration worried me next day and even before Reveille I was up and inspecting the unsightliness in my shaving mirror. We raised some talcum powder and we did our best with that. Even so, B.S.M. Greenaway spotted the disfigurement at early morning stables as, of course, he would. He chose to be jocular about it, however, and that afforded a measure of relief.

"Well, Cadet Lamont: been out last night with Henry Ainley?"

There was a hidden barb in that sally for Ainley was, indeed, a fellow cadet and a very popular one at that, but however gifted an actor he undoubtedly was his skill in the saddle could scarcely be described as equally great. For some reason or other, unknown to everyone, he was the butt for the B.S.M.'s most caustic gibes. I think it was probably that the untutored fellow had the firm con-

B

viction that in civilian life Ainley was a well-known comedian and, therefore, fair game by his reasoning. "You may be funny on the stage, Cadet Ainley, but you're a darn sight funnier on that horse!" I had heard him say.

Anyway, poor Ainley., a few days earlier, had taken rather an ugly fall when we were riding with folded arms and without saddle and irons; he was badly bruised.

Later at 9 a.m. parade I stood rigidly but in fear and trepidation in the middle of the rear rank during the inevitable minute inspection. Horror leaped upon horror when first Cadet McKeown and in turn Cadet Lamont received the order: "Two paces to the rear: backward march: wheel right. To the Orderly Room, walk march!"

Same old route! same old scene! Here comes the end at last! R.T.U. now and for ever, Amen!

This time, though, we were taken in separately; that must be the routine on rejection, thought I.

My movements before the All-Highest were impeccable — clockwork — although I was acutely conscious of my ruby-red beacon proclaiming my ignominy before all the assembled immaculate gallantry.

By some sadistic whim, it appeared to me, Lord Alfred had shed all his air of severity; on the contrary he could have been described as benign.

"Oh, Lamont; I have been looking over your Division Tests. They're very good — you know quite a bit of mathematics, don't you?"

Puzzled at first, as he went on to quiz me about my knowledge of the differential calculus and kindred bafflements, I then began to sense where all this was leading. If I didn't make the grade in my knowledge of maths. he could take the less drastic course to R.T.U. of recommending me to an alternative branch of the Service— Flying Corps, likely as not; they were always sending cadging chits for volunteers; or it might be Toc Emmas.

I proceeded to lay on the maths. theme as hard as I knew how!

Then the startling news broke: "That's just as we thought. War Office want a few cadets with particular aptitude to undergo a special course of gunnery in connection with a new artillery method of sniping mobile targets. I'm putting up McKeown and you from this brigade; I'm sure you'll both do well. Fall out!"

Felix Q and I soon travelled to Maresfield Park in Sussex and then, fully commissioned, to Lydd just landward from Dungeness in Kent for the actual firing which was largely conducted with the comparatively new employment of aerial co-operation.

When the examination results were posted up McKeown topped the list but modesty restrains me from indicating who was runner-up. We were the only two cadets, I must, however, confess, who never were rewarded, prior to our gazetting, with even one single stripe for general deportment.

We returned to France together but parted at Le Havre.

He won well deserved honour and survives today to practise medicine with distinction in the Midlands.

Good old Felix Q!

For myself I came in time to cherish nothing but gratitude towards Lord Alfred's stringencies for I am sure that the discipline and his example contributed in no small measure towards a wonderful experience that eventually it became my proud privilege to earn. At Bordon Camp, Hampshire, where I was stationed long afterwards I was invited to accept seconding as Signals Officer to a superb, newly transformed fighting unit, The Household Cavalry Brigade of Artillery, by its Commander, Colonel the Hon. John (Jacob) Astor, 1st Life Guards, Chevalier de Légion d' Honneur, President of the Press Club, and ultimately Chairman of the Times Publishing Company.

Beyond the recollection of the magnificent leadership of Colonel Astor and the splendid quality of the soldiers, as well it might be, they having obtained their baptism of fire as Life and Horse Guardsmen, I have only dim memory of a Major Sims-Woolley who was credited, perhaps erroneously, with being the prime instigator to train these men as gunners. Cavalry, as such, could not be used on the Western front in the closing year of the war and the day of the Panzer Division to show us the way had not yet arrived; our Royal Tank Corps had its origins in the Machine Gun Corps.

Major Sims-Woolley who had been severely wounded at Mons, losing an arm, had been invalided out, it was said, despite all protests from himself.

Failing to find the employment he craved for in his own country he succeeded in gaining command of a French seventy-five millimetre battery. From the French service he was to be again relegated as unfit. Determined to be anything but idle he propounded the idea which, be the laurels awarded to the Mad Major, as he was known, or not, saw the formation of the illustrious band into which I was so proud to be assimilated and to wear the distinctive red and blue lanyard.

With them I fought in the "Backs to the Wall" action at Amiens, Germany's last desperate assault. To begin with we were without our ordnance and fought as infantry. Amiens held, for which it received the *Croix de Guerre avec Palmes*, like our George Cross Island of Malta in the later war. Then, equipped with seven-inch land-mounted naval guns, the Household Brigade were ripe for participation in Haig's furious and final stroke.

The gunners were truly superb — too superb in their rigid discipline at first; not like my preceding No. 2 Six-inch Howitzer Battery, probably the oldest soldiers in France — they did not wait for the word of command to take cover, under the trail or anywhere else nearby when the hostile rounds began to come in!

After fighting right through the last summer, during which I had the novel experience of firing shrapnel from these hefty pieces over open sights at retreating Germans, we went into rest at Aire. We were billeted in a luxurious and large white *château* which, in a manner quite usual with the French, was on the opposite side of the road from the proprietor's own distillery!

Could the mind of man conjure up the vision of any more delectable a situation in which to wage war? Evidently this owner thought much along these lines for he fussed and ran about continually, making sure that valuable clocks or costly rugs were still where they should be.

He need not have worried! Neither Colonel Astor's officers nor his men even as much noticed his *objets d'art;* they, like me, were more amazed and delighted to know that there existed a world without the louse!

As for the distillery, it was no Naboth's vineyard for the finest troops in all the world.

One night, though, I do recall when a bottle figured conspicuously. There was quite a bit of bombing going on near our billet. A group of little houses close to a railway siding were set alight and the C.O. ordered me to take a small party and make a round, rendering any assistance to the French occupants that might seem to be needed.

We did help a little, carrying buckets to extinguish what were really just minor blazings, moving furniture, soothing kiddies and all the odd chores that go with this sort of thing.

In her gratitude, however, one old French granny delved amongst her *lares* and *penates* and insisted, despite protest from me, in presenting me with a dumpy, cobwebby old bottle filled wih some rubbishy vin rouge, as I thought.

I thought wrongly, however, because I showed it to Colonel Astor who very quickly asked me if, as Mess Secretary, I made a habit of stocking up with this sort of thing; he felt sure that his junior officers would very soon feel the draught if I did!

It was a genuine distillation by the French survivors of the English Novice House of the religious Order of Monks of St. Benedict. Despite that it tasted very good — so Colonel Astor told us anyway!

I have hurdled events very considerably by recalling this happy assimilation into the august company of the Guards. Before it took place I was to have a somewhat variegated career and during the peregrinations this entailed I had, I think, the unique experience of being in action against hostile armed forces of two different nations, not only the one in France, but the other in my own country of Scotland, as will be seen.

The less glorious contact with the Registrar in St. George's Hospital never should have been repeated but there it is, some men will never learn and years later, on return to civilian life, by my own unaided efforts, I brought upon myself precisely the same chagrin and the quite similar not inconsiderable physical pain.

These two mortifying rewards inevitably follow when the two precepts, non-repetition of mistakes and non-interference with a Donna's choice, are treated with less of the respect they merit!

CHAPTER IV

On leaving Felix McKeown I was posted to the First Army for detached duty. Initially this was as Section Commander with four point five Field Howitzers which I was ordered to use for sniping purposes of a harassing nature and, in particular, at any mobile target which presented.

This meant that, at nightfall, we manhandled the pieces from a concealed position up to a point as near to the front line as possible. I generally elected to go myself in the foremost trench and to the dismay of the infantry reluctantly obliged to remain there, proceed to divert myself with a "Dangerous Shoot."

This is one which engages a specific target, say a sniper's post or a machine gun nest, so close to your own side that, with ordinary behaviour, the rounds falling a little short would more than incommode the home team.

There is a special technique by which it is done, with comparative safety to your friends but you, yourself, are dependent for your continued well-being on the accuracy of your mathematical calculations.

If you are lucky and obliterate any such target as I have named you are lauded and fêted by the P.B.I. Should the human error obtrude even just a little bit you are cursed and consigned to the fieriest arsenal catering for reckless gunner officers.

At a place we named Coke Ovens, I spotted my first moving temptation, of all things, a German officer on *horseback*, reading, by the faintest light of first dawn, assisted presumably by a shaded lamp, a large unfolded map. In the joy of having this presented to me and without much thought for the consequences I immediately proceeded to bracket him.

When satisfied I let him have salvo after salvo at a cost to the country of several thousand pounds.

The result was spectacular; the shortish rounds, arriving in no-man's land covered the men on front-line dawn stand-to with much débris and shop-soiled barbed wire of their own implanting; even the parados behind me got it too.

The enemy horseman certainly turned tail but at quite a leisurely pace and, before changing to the trot, came round in his saddle to give a friendy wave of the hand in my direction!

He would not see me, of course, but he was bound to have spotted my gun flashes.

I certainly had it in my heart to admire that man's nerve.

What was more disconcerting, however, was that some Very light enthusiast, in a moment apparently of, possibly, quite justifiable jitters, let fly the S.O.S., two reds and a white; immediately the whole sector was ablaze with ordnance firing at the imagined dawn attack from over the way.

Being a sniper on special duty I felt myself at liberty to fold my tent, like the Arabs, and silently steal away.

Thus I missed the Battalion Commander's far from benign envoi which, I learned later, was a perfect beauty.

Neither was I ever invited to pay another call.

My next assignment was attended by much heartier applause, encomiums, in fact, which I received with complete and nonchalant aplomb, conveying the impression that they were no more than my just and lawful reward for careful planning and cunning execution.

I was switched to the temporary command of a single railway-mounted eleven-inch Howitzer.

On arrival at the battery site I found that the most senior surviving rank was the Sergeant-Major. The position was being attacked many times each day with a concentrated counter-battery shoot by at least one full German brigade.

The Battery Commander, killed that day, was still awaiting removal from his dug-out.

All other officers had become casualties.

The prospect was not particularly inviting but I made haste to look over the maps, the aiming posts, registered targets and all the printed tables applicable to the working of this mammoth beside which my own original thirteen-pounder weapons would have been less than children's pop-guns.

Accompanied by the B.S.M. I left the B.C. post and inspected the gun site; every available detail was working with utmost speed to alter bits and pieces of the painted fragments of canvas, woven into the immense erection of wire-netting over Gargantua.

This constituted the vast canopy of a camouflage device and the eagerness of the Sergeant-Major to leave the B.C. post and come here was explained now by the fervour with which he began to exhort all to "get on with them alterations; a spotting plane will take his photograph at any moment now.

"You don't want them to know we're not knocked out yet, div you?"

Herculean efforts in response gave clear evidence that the law of self-preservation was still extant here and that the key to its observance was the green and brown rag-festooned contraption.

A signaller delivered the summons from Brigade H.Q.; I was required immediately to engage a specific target with forty rounds of the immense projectiles.

The objective was a registered one and the shoot would be without observation.

I applied myself diligently to my table of corrections, temperature, wind deflection, drift, wear of gun and all the rest.

I checked them over carefully and, satisfied, gave the order to commence firing.

B.S.M. on the gun-site acted as Section Commander and relayed my commands.

The roar of detonation was music to a gunner officer's ears; not so pleasing to his eyes was the huge conflagration with mighty volumes of dense white smoke that accompanied it. Towers of flame licked the heavens; crackling canvas ripped and cavorted with a sharp-shooter's staccato.

For miles around, the display of pyrotechnics must have evoked sympathetic voicings by the wise; "Hello, an ammunition dump gone up over there! Poor devils, those who were near it."

The layer of my monster cannon and his mate had not lost time in any way; they took a flying leap at the first outburst of fireworks, and had safely joined the B.S.M. at his self-appointed place to the rear by the time a really decent show was on.

When the eyes of all personnel were tired of smoke and flames they turned, quite balefully, to gaze in my direction; I did not need to guess what profanities were being hurled by the entire company at my abashed tin-hatted head.

The calculations that I had made were perfect; the trouble was that there was one I had not made at all!

The angle of elevation was such as must bring the diligently contrived "them alterations" of the sun-dried canvas rags directly within the influence of the blast; hence these tears, caused not only by the smoke and fire, but the awareness that "Big Bella" now reared her massive snout in a state of complete nudity. What an opportunity for the first Peeping Tom of a Hun reconnaissance plane!

My name was mud. There was talk of evacuating the gun-site; "He'll need to phone Brigade an' get permission for the loco to come up and change position. We're in for it now, the stupid, blundering idiot . . . ." and so on ad lib.

The B.S.M. who could scarcely bring himself to address me at first, then changed round and kept me well-informed as to the near-mutinous state of collapsed morale.

But we Celtic sibs are made of sterner stuff; the scion of the Lamont of Lamont said nothing at all.

A whine overhead, identified by the spotter at the Lewis gun as " 'ostile hairyplane a 'overing hover'ead" was the tocsin for him and his opposite number of the other flank to swivel round and prepare to fire aloft.

"Hold fast, Battery Protection! Do not fire; Battery, all lie down and do not move one inch! Battery Sergeant-Major, see to it or I'll have the lot of you put under close arrest for abandoning your posts when ordered to engage the enemy!"

I hurled my cannonade at them. Stunned silence greeted it but they obeyed to a man.

Jerry by now was close at hand; some distant Ack Ack guns were firing busily at him. The white powder puffs of their bursts were all over the sky, as far away from the target as were their initiators.

He soared immediately above us, circled three times with, no doubt, his Zeiss lenses working overtime.

In quite leisurely fashion he took a right good gander, then returned to the Fatherland where presumably his pictures would be developed with all dispatch.

I gave him just time to consume enough petrol to ensure there was no chance of his coming back for a space.

"Battery; action!"

Horror in the men's faces greeted this order.

"Harassing fire — three nine-rounds on elevation and deflection as ordered before."

"Fire!"

In a kind of dumbly confounded state of amazement they went to their posts.

The shoot was completed.

"Battery Sergeant-Major; cease firing. Prepare gun for immediate action on S.O.S. aiming post. Then battery fall in for address by Commander. Move!"

I had by now been doing a bit of solid thinking, not too soon, it may justifiably be thought.

I reasoned thus: ordinarily a Hun airman, unless he thought it an utter futility, would have squeezed the tits and let us have some bursts from his own machine guns. I could only conclude that this chap was satisfied that no living thing, capable of being exterminated, existed here below.

With the men paraded I began: "You lot belong to siege artillery; that was fine at Omdurman or such places if a set of dog-gone ignoramuses such as yourselves ever heard of it. This war requires artillery, real artillery, not a crowd of garrison wallahs more used to a bathing marquee on the beach at Brighton.

"You've had a rough time; nobody denies it, but of all the

damnfool, nonsensical, stupid idiotic ideas, to think that a camera in a German spotter aeroplane wouldn't instantly pick out that vivid pepper and salt you mugs thought was camouflage and which *I had to dispose of effectively before the sun sets* . . . . words fail me to tell you what I think of you!"

Truth to tell words had failed me for I was wondering where I went from there.

Then, with sudden inspiration, I roared on, hoping all the time, that there was not among their number anyone with the slightest knowledge of mineralogy.

"What do you see in front of you, behind you, all around you, if siege gunners are capable of seeing at all which I very much doubt?

"Ferruginous soil, you mugs, sand-stone stuff, rusty brown in colour with clumps of black.

"What have I, with prompt and considered action, left you with on your gun-site? Look, you blighters, look!

"Is it not a perfect blend — the charred remains of your stupidity, I mean?

"You will go off, stand-to when I order it but I can tell you this much; when you go to roost this night you can close your eyes and I admit that it will be the first time for long enough, but go to sleep, knowing that not one hostile round will ever enter this battery position again.

"Battery-Sergeant-Major; dismiss the parade!"

I argued that if events proved me wrong there would be nobody left alive to denounce me; if I were to be correct I might as well have a bit of kudos even for something I hadn't done; I seldom got much of the commodity for things I *had* done.

As far as I am informed not a single shot has landed there, since that blaze of mine, not up until this moment anyway.

* * * * *

The B.S.M. came over to the B.C.'s dug-out at midnight as arranged. I had but newly finished the most difficult letter of its kind that I'd ever had to indite.

"Who makes up your returns, Sergeant-Major?"

"Sergeant Sherwood, Sir; he's Acting Orderly Room Clerk just now."

"Very good; tell him it's to go in as 'Killed in Action' Church of England. By the way, thanks for sending over the No. 2 Field Dressing: it covered up everything on his head.

"You can move off for the cemetery any time now; I saw the three-ton lorry come up. You haven't any Catholics going with the party I hope, Sergeant-Major?"

"As a matter of fact I'm Catholic myself, Sir."

"Oh, B.S.M.; I'm sorry: I did not know. Tell me straight out if you'd prefer not to go along. I'll quite understand. I know that people of your faith have certain scruples about this sort of thing."

His glance was steady and his voice firm; "Thank you, Sir; I can't say as 'ow I like the idea of travelling along of the lorry but it's my duty and I mean to see it through."

"Good man, B.S.M. And it's agreed that mum's the word for all time?"

"That's what I think it should be too, Sir; I give you my word."

"Right, B.S.M. Night-night to you."

"Goodnight, Sir, and thank you for what you've done for him."

I rolled over in my flea--bag on the wire-netting mattress of the bunk. Sleep wasn't very far away but before I snuffed the candle I took a last look at where he had lain in the dug-out; then I glanced up at the earthy side, to the stick on which I had slung the holster containing his revolver.

No need for anyone else in the world to know that from the cartouche, fixed to my own body-belt, I had but recently extracted a single live round and replaced the expended shell in his Webley with it.

All was neat and tidy now: I dowsed the glim.

All the same, County Cricket had lost a first-class bat but what was more important than that, I mused as sleep overcame, not the slightest hint was left that could ever hurt the widow.

*　*　*　*　*

Still enjoying the nomadic life on special duties I next found myself as Second in Command of a sixteen-pounder Field Artillery battery, the 1st/1st London.

My sojourn with them was not long. When taking cover one night in a cellar with a party of my signallers and a medical officer, whilst under bombardment, we got a shower of mustard gas mixed up with the high explosive.

Having barely time to register the conviction that I had gulped down Mr Colman's entire factory I passed into oblivion. Most of the others were killed, I learned later.

The Base Hospital at Le Havre was as far as I needed to go back for active treatment; then someone with the bowels of compassion in his make-up deflected me from there, after a further short stay, to the lovely russet-brown lanes and orchards of Sussex, near the market town of Horsham.

Officially I was on a Battery Commander's course but I was obviously one old soldier and a bit part-worn at that. So I was left in peace and the instructors turned a blind eye to my empty chair in the lecture hut; I used it only now and then when the weather was not too good.

I recall in the passing that we welcomed there the first artillery contingent of our oldest allies to come over here.

It was in that Mess, too, that, with my own eyes, I read the Army Council Instruction which, without the slightest pulling of its punches, peremptorily forbade all ranks to employ the usual designation, "Bloody Pork and Beans" which was the unkind thrust of Thomas Atkins at these men of ancient exploration valour.

In their favour, I do recall that they had a lovely band: in numbers it must have quite equalled the operationally effective details.

The officers wore epaulettes of gold and carried swords.

On the day following this ornamental influx I made a point of parading for gun-drill; it was an established practice for all British officers to remove tunics, roll up sleeves and lend a hand with the moving of the guns which were manned by other ranks attached to the school.

When it came to the turn of our newly arrived visitors, their officers, in no uncertain terms, refused to follow suit.

That was the basis of their unpopularity, at any rate, in Horsham. The *debâcle* in front of Aire, in France, where the 51st (Highland) Division happened to be out on rest when ordered suddenly to return and re-occupy the sector of abruptly abandoned front-line, is one over which it were best to draw a veil ("Look, Jock, thon's bluidy Germans with their blue uniforms; let the b——s have it!")

Pleasant and balmy as Horsham was it was not evidently just what the doctor ordered in regard to my mustard-seasoned tubes; the wheezes and the what-nots, like Johnnie Walker, were still going strong! No one will ever convince me that there are not wise and gentle people in the Army for, to my great delight and astonishment, I received a temporary posting to a Coast Defence Battery, Ardhallow Fort, located, by all the sacred bones of my ancestors, at no less an Elysium than the River Clyde and, at that, only some five miles from our home, Gowanlea, in Innellan.

Banzai!

It took but two months of fragrant Bullwood air, even with all its myriads of attendant midges (better than lice, though!) to disperse my bronchial expostulations but in that brief time I enjoyed two episodes which are still quite fresh in my mind.

CHAPTER V

The C.R.A. in charge of Clyde Defences had his H.Q. right across the estuary at the Cloch Lighthouse. I forget his name but the old hands I met all referred to him as "Hooks."

He was not altogether a popular Commander, why, I did not know but I certainly detected two idiosyncrasies in him; one was a complete allergy to the presence of any dogs in a battery and the other was an irascibility of nature to which he gave full vent when he saw, or thought he saw, any evidence of loafing.

In Ardhallow Fort the B.C. lived out; the Second in Command was, like my mother, a Stewart. He was the son of another Lord Provost of Glasgow and himself became a baronet, a highly respected and eminent man of affairs in the West of Scotland.

There came a time when target practice on the wide Firth was the order of the day, and Captain Stewart elected to board the tug-boat and undertake the duties of Target Officer himself. I assumed his place in the B.C. post to control the firing from the heavy armament.

It may sound a little boastful coming from a Horse Gunner but the Depression Range Finder, completely differing from field apparatus, presented no terrors from the very start of my first calibration shoot. This was because, at this time, I was deeply immersed in theoretical gunnery and was indeed experimenting with some ideas of my own.

The weather was warm and sunny; far out on the broad expanse of the Firth of Clyde, abeam the Islands of Cumbrae, we could see the towing vessel going slowly ahead, the twin check-patterned targets afloat on their rafts far astern at different spacings of distance.

Through my powerful observation glasses I could see that Jimmie Stewart, wise man, was improving the shining hour by quietly taking things easy; he had a deck chair rigged aft on the tug and, to all appearances, was nicely fast asleep thereupon.

Now, quite unknown to the slumberer, Colonel "Hooks" had paid the battery an altogether unexpected visit. "I shall watch you take the shoot, Captain Lamont, but, at any time, I may declare you a casualty, when next in seniority will act as Battery Commander;" was his order.

Beside me, in our protected point of vantage above the emplacements, he waited impatiently for the start.

"What's that Target Officer thinking of? Why doesn't he pass the signal to commence firing?" he demanded.

Wondering how on earth I could warn poor old Stewart of his peril, I temporised: "No doubt he's waiting for some shipping we can't see to clear the danger zone, Sir."

"Stuff and nonsense, there's no shipping! Signaller! Call the target-ship, and ask the officer on board what he thinks he's playing at;" "Hooks" directed incontinently.

Signals, down below, did as he was bid; from my perch I watched the reactions out at sea.

A pad was presented to our Target Officer after he had been aroused by some not-too-gentle shoulder shaking and he scribbled his reply.

I commenced to read it out, as it blinked through in Morse, to myself.

I held my breath and waited; no loyal gunner would let his Second in Command down, I felt quite sure. To be certain I leaned over the ledge of my concrete eyrie and shouted: "Signaller; pass your message to the Master Gunner to bring here."

This would give the non-commssioned officer time to do a bit of censoring. So I thought!

To my horror, on arrival, he read the thing out in its entirety.

It was addressed to me: "Trying to catch some bloody oysters without hooks."

In a strained, tense silence preparation for ranging went on.

In a slight lull between the terrific reverberation there was a sudden crash of broken glass, coming from the small tool shed, to the left flank, just outside the defensive perimeter of the Battery.

Through a smashed window dashed our six panic-stricken, fine pets; their leader, in full cry, was a particular favourite of mine, a smooth-haired Irish terrier. The agonised animal, its silken sheen entirely debauched, his sensitive muzzle lacerated and bloody, was running amok.

"Who was the fool that put the dogs in there during a shoot?" I roared, putting down my glasses and letting the fall of rounds go to pot.

Battery Commander's Assistant, by my side, answered: "Master Gunner's orders, Sir."

"Hooks" was livid. He glared at me but he was momentarily speechless.

At last: "What do you mean by this Captain Lamont? How dare you take your eyes off the target? There will be a Court of Inquiry about those dogs: I suppose by your actions one is yours.

I declare you a casualty; leave the Battery Commander's Post — at once!"

"Only sensible order you're given today;" I shouted back at him as I raced to find Sexton, the batman, to help me soothe the hysterical dogs.

On my flight I heard No. 1 of the nearest gun hail me with a cry: "C.R.A.'s calling you back, Sir."

"Tell him I'm away for some oysters, the old B.F.!"

I did not go near him and not again in my life did I ever see him. What the aftermath was I knew not nor cared.

All I resolved was that I had it in for that Master Gunner, as soon as the opportunity was given me.

That was not long delayed.

* * * * *

It was surely the most dramatic invasion Old Father Clyde could have seen since the Battle of Largs in all his long, splendid history.

I was taking my ease in the Mess when it happened.

The first call was an Alert from H.Q., C.R.A.:

"Hostile warship with five funnels approaching Boom Defences Dunoon at speed Stop Prepare for action Stop Stand by to engage Stop Report when ready Stop Do not fire until ordered Stop message ends."

I yawned when I read it from the pad: "Oh, there he goes again! More of old "Hook's" trial runs but why he made it a packet of Woodbine the good Lord only knows."

The name I gave the ship, of course, referred to the five-cigarette containing carton then popular with the troops; it stuck and it is what all those who were there invariably employ in mentioning that vessel. The real title was much too difficult to remember; it sounded to me like *Ascaris* but then I recalled, from my zoological studies, that this was a genus of parasitical worms of the intestine and that did not seem to be the sort of name her original designers would fancy.

We first saw her abreast of Innellan; the searchlights, established by our Sappers beside the statue of Highland Mary in Castle Gardens, West Bay, Dunoon ("Queen of Watering Places") caught and held her, the silhouetted acme of black sinistrality.

The bone in her teeth, no less than the luminous cream of her wake, were companioned by five swept-back eruptions of dense black smoke and gave visible indication of the high triple-screw revolutions.

In her mad career she was driving close inshore towards the inevitable destruction of the defence boom spanning the Firth from Dunoon to the Cloch.

I followed and kept her with a steep declination on the D.R.F. and could have blown her right out of the water any moment, would "Hooks" but give the word of command we all longed for.

No order came.

To our dismay the whirling screws, threshing the air as her bows buried deep with the impact of the boom, slewed her right round and she stopped, a great long snake of dark armed menace.

By now we had learned from signal exchanges that she was identified as a Russian warship; she had ignored all orders to stop from the moment she rounded the Mull of Kintyre, emerging from the recesses of Atlantic wastes and heading for the Clyde.

Certainly, she was trailed all the way but why they did not allow us to warn at least with one shot across the bows I never understood; it would have saved the disconsolate Boom Defence Officer a great deal of headache.

There could have been no diplomatic repercussions for she was manned by Bolsheviki, a mutinous crew sworn to attack all bourgeosi, who had put their captain and executive officers in irons. Over and above that and her defiance of orders in British home waters this country had but newly decided at this time to occupy Archangel and district with an expeditionary force.

The next development was a call from Dunoon Burgh Police; a landing party, presumably offensive, had come ashore and when challenged could neither understand nor be understood.

It was gathered that a number of the good folk of the popular seaside resort had taken to the hills in the hinterland. An armed party from Ardhallow Fort was requested forthwith.

The men were available but to arm them was another matter. Apart from the battery protection of one heavy Vickers machine gun there were, according to the armourer, but six rifles with bayonets and, in addition, three others of the latter, quite unattached.

I wondered at the presence of the spare parts and mentally concluded that someone had been up to his nonsense and I thought I knew who was probably the villain. At any rate the arms were badly oiled and for that offence the Master Gunner was ordered to accompany the portly stockbroker, a temporary subaltern doing his bit, and proceed at the double to the scene of operations.

With sudden vision there was added to the punitive party a Polish gunner whom I had come across some days back, a man on the run, I had suspected.

He was, however, to save the day as interpreter; the objective of the Bolshies proved to be hard liquor which they sought by breaking into the first public house they encountered.

Old Hancock, the patrol leader, never hesitated; he used force with a minimum of parley and held the lot until the Navy took over.

The orders were that, after conclusion of the mission, the party was to return leaving behind the Master Gunner who would stay until it was ensured that all was settled and quiet.

When it was notified that Hancock's men were on the way home I strolled over to the left flank of the battery to examine the Vickers; thinking back to the small arms I was gratified that this weapon was decently tended.

Then, cheated of a crack at "Packet of Woodbine," I thought it would cheer things up a bit all round if I gave a few bursts down on to the slopes of grass now glistening dewily in the dawn light.

I called for a belt and fed it in myself.

Soon the small expeditionary force was ascending well within my arc of fire; I witheld all action for the moment.

Then the inspiration of the entire night really clicked: I waited.

The battery now had orders to stand easy in my rear for instructional purpose in Machine Gun Protection.

The last report had come in; the situation in Dunoon was completely resolved and our Master Gunner was returning by transport to Ardhallow gates. Could sentry please be warned?

He certainly could! But trust that blighter to scrounge anything that was going, even a lift!

He came toiling up the gradual slope of the broad green expanse.

Getting a distinctive brown patch about twelve inches to his right flank into my sights I let it have a nice prolonged burst.

Rat-a-tat, tat, tat, tat; rat-a-tat, tat, tat.

It was music to the ears of the mitrailleur, certified marksman of the Scottish Brigade of Yeomanry and a lover of dogs!

To the eyes of a non-commissioned officer, knowledgeable like anything as a barrack-room lawyer, the sprouting fronds of earth beside him and the invisibility of his murderer were all the horrors of hell; this was quite different from the dangers he had, quite irregularly, been forced to meet that night.

"Here's one for Pongo;" I addressed no one in particular as I named the flight-leader of the recent doggie sortie, engendered by the panic-making detonations of a battery in action.

At first my assembled audience to the rear were horror-striken; they probably thought they had a certified lunatic in their midst.

"This one's for Whipsey; that for Betty and just to brighten your life, here's a good one for Towser."

The commentary synchronised with individual bursts, first to both flanks of the khaki figure now, quite reasonably, lying prone on the ground; to his front, twelve inches from his nose, then, for good measure, just above his head. (It was the method by which

C

I had been trained to keep my own brain-box down, by the way, and, in former days, I had often been called upon to do such firing).

The last bit of the belt clipped the tree branches up top and let in more of the daylight.

I was enjoying myself hugely; I took to sending messages of some obscenity, all with loves and kisses, to my prostrate target, in the Morse Code.

Rat-a-tat, rat-a-tat, rat-a-tat. Tat, tat, tat — tat, tat, tat, tat, — tat, tat — rat-tat, rat-tat, rat-tat.

This practice was one we had started at Barrie Camp Musketry and Machine Gun Course but one which had been frowned upon by Authority in France when we took to communicating to the Huns our innermost thoughts on the validity of their parents' wedding, with the stutters of an automatic weapon.

The signallers blew the gaff to the others at Ardhallow and the battery became convulsed with laughter. When my belt was all but exhausted and it would soon jam anyway, I decided he had had enough; and I gave him the final CI, VE; "Come in Stop Message ends."

He wouldn't move though and so nice, kind-hearted Stock-broker Hancock once more, on that tour of duty, descended the green slopes to escort him to his hide-out and smooth the man's ruffled plumage.

One thing more remained to be done. This was the outcome of a precept learned by me in the Field Reconnaissance Unit: "Always secure your rear against attack." Even to this day, I remember this injunction but, at times, I must confess, lamentably fail to comply with it until too late.

Calling up the gunners I gave them a brief talk on dismantling and cleaning — then left them to do it all.

In the Orderly Room immediately thereafter I made appropriate entry in the ledger for consumption of lethal missiles.

"Ammunition, Expenditure of, nature, date and operation. Authority for same."

I appended the legend as follows to the entry of two hundred odd rounds, .303 ammo.

"O.A.S. (On Active Service — I thought "Hooks" would appreciate that pointed reminder!)

"Advantage taken of unusual Alert stand-by order emanating C.R.A.'s office, to give realistic background to instructional exercise for Vickers Machine Gun crew in covering and corrective fire by controlled arc at offensive target. (Signed) D.L., R.H.A. (attached)."

It was a bit windy, I thought, but I got rid of my spleen.

It was as well that I did so, as it transpired, for the makings of a fine further Court of Inquiry blew up.

Curiously enough, there was no corroboration forthcoming from any other ranks for the aggrieved Master Gunner's averments.

The "Packet of Woodbine" lay in the sheltered anchorage of the Holy Loch nearby for many years, I think until well after the nineteen twenties.

The Bolsheviki were all confined, so the five-funnelled P.O.W.'s mobocracy of a crew became, indeed, P.O.W.'s of another kind.

It is a coincidence that this place of anchorage for this rebel ship in the Holy Loch now became the base for the American Polaris Missile Mother Ship and her brood of submarines — U.S. Navy Ship Proteus.

CHAPTER VI

The halcyon days at Ardhallow soon drew to a close. There followed advanced courses of telegraphy at Dunfermline under the direction of Post Office instructors. There I first learned how to design and fashion a field telephone exchange. The particular feature of my prototype was that I could "Marry" a land line to wireless telegraphy receivers, crude affairs by modern standards. The device enabled direct contact between the observer of a co-operating aeroplane and the battery. The system is called "linking" nowadays and it can be used with the radio telephone. I came to use the method extensively in the technique of medical aid to ships at sea by radio transmission.

* * * * *

Following upon embarkation leave after Dunfermline I was to see action next in the hell-wracked morass of Passchendaele Ridge. Whilst Forward Observation Officer for the artillery brigade supporting the Hawk Battalion of the Naval Division I was pretty badly mauled in some hand to hand fighting at a place we called Inch Houses; in reality, all of man-made construction to be viewed there was a derelict tank; the remainder of the scene was comprised of human destruction and mud.

With another officer, who was in command, and a party of ten signallers we went over the top at dawn; it was the bloodiest day of all the fighting I ever saw. Two of the signallers and I were the sole survivors of our little party; even my carrier pigeons and their handler were annihilated. No officers of A Company, who were part of the first wave and with which we attacked, ever returned.

My two men were subsequently decorated with the Military Medal for carrying me in through the quagmire when darkness had fallen.

Ultimately and for the second time I became a patient in No. 3 General Hospital in Wandsworth; twenty-four hours later my brother from Innellan visited me and whilst I was naturally overjoyed to see him I did not much relish the transparent reason for his having been summoned to my bed-side that first morning.

Later on in the day I could barely discern a very tall, largely built lady in the uniform of the V.A.D. moving from bed to bed; my eyes seemed to be riveted on the bright yellow shoes she wore.

In time she came to me and sat down; about her there was, I thought, something of a great dignity. Her eyes, dark, lustrous and tender had sadness in them too. She spoke with a foreign intonation that was bewitching, and she was extremely kind and gentle with me; quite unostentatiously she left a little packet of acid drops on my locker. Day after day she returned and I looked forward to her coming; she would ask no fulsome questions as to how I was feeling but was just soothing in some intangible way — a motherly person, I sensed.

One day, when the effort of conversing was coming more easily to me she inquired if I could explain the meaning of a quaint phrase she had caught from someone else in the ward. The puzzling expression used had been "dirty dog."

I did my best with many expansive Teutonic examples.

"Eh bien," and those wonderful eyes were alight; "my uncle then is what you call a 'dirty dog'!"

"You'll be the best judge," I answered. "What's he been up to?"

"He has joined himself with the Bosche!"

"And who might he be when he's at home?"

"He is the King of Bulgaria — Ferdinand!"

And you, Madame, if I may ask?"

"I am Queen Amelia."

The information conveyed little to me then but I soon learned that here indeed was the courageous exiled Queen of Portugal who had interposed herself between the assassin and her son to take the bullet herself. Now at Wandsworth, in circumstances anything but opulent, she could not do enough for the men in that ward which she had adopted.

All of us came to love her; every eye was wont to gaze on the large massive frame in real affection and there always was especial regard for the brightly shining pair of yellow shoes!

Two other visitors came to see me and I was glad to welcome both although the news brought to me by one of them seared my very soul at the time.

The first was Miss Winifred MacBride, an accomplished violinist of considerable concert platform distinction; she happened to be the sister of our very own Cupid MacBride, one of the original University students to enlist in the Lanarkshire Yeomanry with me.

The other caller was my battery commander, Major Cameron, on leave from France.

After solicitous inquiry as to my well-being, in rather hesitant fashion he imparted something which was the cause of my disquietude.

"I'm terribly sorry, Dan, but your M.C. is not to be allowed to go through after all. I put you up all right for, according to the infantry, your barrage control was wonderfully good considering the awful conditions. Brigade supported it but the General won't pass it — says you took unwarrantable risks by going over with the first wave; you should have been behind the infantry, he says, according to your orders."

"Good heavens, Sir," I opened out; "has he any idea of what the ground was like? There wasn't one single solid duckboard within miles for the Huns' barrage made a complete square; the only chance for any visual signalling was to be well up to them and I had even got to that machine gun post you engaged when the infantry boys were wiped out leaving me with nothing but Germans and mud to face!"

"I know, I know, Old Boy, but you must remember what the Butcher's like; he said it was certainly quite good the way you fought your way out; he's let the mention go through but according to him, you should have been using a cable line and needn't have led your men so far forward."

"Cable!" I snorted in disgust; "how on earth does he think we could have kept any line repaired in that quagmire? I don't believe he's ever seen the Ridge!"

"Neither do I, Dan. The whole thing's a damned shame; you weren't even in command. By the way, I may tell you now that nothing of the other officer has been found; he must either have been blown to bits or just swallowed up in the swamp."

Needless to say this intelligence served to deepen my depression but what was really worrying me was not the missing of the decoration, although I admitted that would have been a nice thing for the family's sake. What injured me deeply was the unjustified imputation that I was responsible for the loss of my men.

I have seen this many, many times in my life since then; the harshest critics of a soldier are always those who work on theory, not action.

*   *   *   *   *

It was two months later before I received my transfer not to the Glasgow hospital for which I had applied, but to the convalescent depot at South Camp, Ripon, and this I considered to be very unfair treatment. Already simmering with resentment over the Passchendaele criticism my feelings were now more bitter than ever. I was placed in Grade D which meant that I paraded for Roll Call in the morning and thereafter my exercise was limited to the slow pacing of some two hundred yards within the confines of the camp.

Ripon was out of bounds, as was Harrogate, for us weaklings. There was nothing whatsoever to do but sit in the Mess; unheard of was anything in the nature of Occupational Therapy; entertainments were unknown. The entry *Recreation* certainly appeared in

Daily Orders but was a complete myth. No leave was allowed and whilst we were well enough fed we were virtually in a prisoners of war cage.

Other officers, like myself, were, I could see, deteriorating psychologically all the time; quarrelling and profanity were the predominant features of life at South Camp as the result of the inept organisation — or lack of it.

After one month of this I was desperate and indeed mutinous. When all my requests for transfer or, alternatively, upgrading had been ignored I made up my mind to provoke a crisis.

Deliberately I tore from my shoulder straps the yellow flashes which were the distinguishing marks of my lowly status. Then I walked out of the camp and made my way to the cathedral which I entered to find solace in the serene tranquility of a stall.

Later, in my new-found freedom, I was enjoying a sight-seeing stroll round the market place when I was fortunate in running into a schoolmate, Arthur Browning, then an officer in the Gordon Highlanders, stationed somewhere in the vicinity.

Arthur had been captain when I was a senior prefect and he was later to play wing-three-quarter for Scotland. He had the longest stride I ever saw in anyone of medium build and to tackle that man on the touchline as he pounded along towards goal was a feat of considerable magnitude. On this occasion in Ripon I literally embraced him in ecstasy and we spent a hilarious evening together.

I walked back that night having had more good done to me by a few hours in a fellow Scot's company than a year of South Camp ever could have achieved!

Next day I waited, grimly hopeful. There was, however, no sign of any disciplinary action being taken so I paraded before the M.O and demanded medical boarding. I was not really fit I knew, but I maintained with vigour that I was and just before the New Year my desire was met; they graded me A. This was really a monstrous affair, jumping a man from totally unfit to fully recovered but it was, after all, where all my scheming had been designed to lead me and this I acknowledged.

Leave for ten days was forthcoming, to date from 31st December. Good, thought I, I can move off early and be home just in time for Ne'erday, dear to the heart of every Scotsman.

At Ripon station, however, I was to learn how wrong was this assumption; I was told that there was an order that no troops were to travel by train for leave purposes on New Year's Day owing to congestion of *essential* freight! Lloyd George himself was credited with the ukase.

There was no service, it seemed, that could fetch me to Scotland before midnight but I'll try it anyway, I thought, determined to board the first northward bound train that came in.

This plan proved abortive; an A.P.M. brusquely refused to allow me on the platform. Very well, then, I retorted, I shall go to Leeds. No use! My warrant said Glasgow and I might as well accept it, I could not travel anywhere.

That's what the A.P.M. thought but I had other ideas and marching out of the station I cast around for the road to Darlington. It wasn't long till I found what I wanted and was bowling along towards the north on an army truck. My valise had had perforce to be left behind temporarily.

At Darlington my inquiries were much more discreet than they had been at Ripon. The platform for the Scots express, I saw in my preliminary reconnaissance, was alive with Red Caps. I thought I could out-manoeuvre them, however, and I loitered in the background till the train's departure was imminent. Then, poised and ready at the ticket collector's gate, I waited for the whistle.

Timed to a nicety, I made my bound and gained the guard's van immediately on that worthy man's heels.

There were shouts and whistles, of course, but the train was on the move and I was in it. The guard was unaware of anything wrong at the moment so he took no steps to stop the train; had he done so I verily believe that, such was the violence of my mood after all that had transpired, I would have floored him. He merely inquired if I had a warrant and on my affirmative reply conducted me through the train to a comfortable seat where I promptly fell asleep from sheer exhaustion.

They were waiting for me at Carlisle; sinister red head-gear abounded in the station as before and one of the wearers came straight at me. "The Assistant Provo-Marshal's compliments, Sir; would you kindly come this way?"

There could of course be no arguing with that but it turned out to be a bit of subterfuge. They had telephoned about me from Darlington right enough, but it was not the A.P.M. who was responsible for the ironical politeness but the Railway Transport Officer. Just the same I was not to be deterred when he put it to me in friendly but decisive tones: "Look here, you old sweat, if you cause any more trouble like this you'll be liable to arrest and court-martial. You'd be far better just to accept things and stay put. Anyway, you are not going on board that or any other train; you can take that order as final!"

Now, from Carlisle to Glasgow is ninety-four miles as the crow flies and I had no desire to hitch-hike that distance, but to Glasgow I was fanatically determined to go for my Ne'erday. Besides, by now I was in a state of overt war of a private nature against authority.

The first step was to purchase a bottle of strong Congo Red solution with which I had become entirely familiar in the chemistry classes. Then, in the lavatory of the Station Hotel, I took from my haversack the bundle of dressings I carried for the protection of some delicate and still tender scars in my groin into which the serrated bayonet of a soon to be deceased German had been deflected. Some of the bundle I applied about my person with a little sprinkling of darkened red chemical as evidence of soiling; another wad I soaked with liberality and squeezed it out over the pan. It all made a presentable gory mess, if not just quite true to life for any over-discriminative eye, but the mischance of meeting such just had to be risked.

I then made my way to the big General Hospital and soon found my objective, the casualty department.

I gambled on the routine here being similar to that of St. George's and, with satisfaction, I presently found myself in a kind of dispensary with a nurse in attendance but no doctor as yet. Still more acceptably I took in with a glance the soiled dressings bucket in a corner.

"Oh, Sister," I apologised with a show of diffidence; "I'm so sorry to trouble you but could you spare me some dressing material? The whole supply I brought along with me from hospital is soaked through."

Thus dissembling and walking with a bit of a limp I quite casually dropped my pseudo-gory dressings in the bucket and took care that the bloody evidence was not too much exposed to view.

She followed every move with a calm and assured professional eye. "What has gone wrong?"

"Oh, nothing much; just this inguinal wound. I think I've strained things a bit by doing too much moving about today. I heard them call it a dissecting aneurism of my femoral artery at No. 3 General Hospital; I'm just out of there, you see."

I was gratified to note that her eyes did then betray a somewhat startled expression.

"Just *out* of hospital! You look to me as if you should just be being *admitted* to hospital; can you manage to get up on the couch and let me see before I call Doctor?"

Whilst undoing my attire for the inspection I was careful, with some manly, well controlled wincing and lip biting, to allow all my other sundry evidences of war injury to be revealed.

"You're surely never having to do all those dressings yourself?" she questioned.

"Oh, no," I reassured her; "I'm on my way to Glasgow and am going to report at the military wing of the Sick Children's Hospital at Yorkhill; I'm on sick leave."

After a close inspection of my thigh she said rather doubtfully but still, I felt, with warm sympathy in her voice. "These gashes aren't bleeding at all now."

"Are they not?" I peered up apprehensively from the mackintosh-covered pillow; "It's liable to come away in spurts."

"Oh, I see; that's quite understandable."

I breathed a heartfelt sigh of relief at that declaration of hers but all the same I did feel a bit of a cad.

The Casualty Surgeon was called, of course, and I went through my piece all over again. I was well versed in the classics, and knew full well the Greeks' use of meiosis, the quality of understatement. This I exploited to the maximum.

The young doctor, apparently but newly qualified, was sympathetic and anxious to do his best for me.

"You're very white in the face, you know. It looks to me as if you ought to stop in here till we see if anything is going to pop off again. Was there much bleeding — Staff-Nurse said something about soakage?"

"There wasn't much on that pad over there but the earlier ones were different." Then I went on hurriedly as his glance strayed to the bucket. "But, Doctor, I must really push on to Glasgow. It's vital to me that I get there by tomorrow — urgent in fact — illness at home. I've not been there for a long time, you see."

I tried to inject a little pathos into this part but I was not convinced that it bore any fruit.

"I don't much like the idea of your bumping about in trains with that sort of intermittent haemorrhage going on," said the doctor. "You haven't anyone with you, have you?"

On being answered he made up his mind and, honest fellow that he was, declared: "Look here; I don't really know much about war wounds; you're really a case for the military registrar. If you'll dress that up with firm bandaging, Staff-Nurse, I shall 'phone him — he's busy down at the railway station at the moment."

Whilst the dressing proceeded I kept my fingers crossed. Exactly how things were to pan out I had no idea, but I was playing my luck and it held.

"You're in clover," announced the youthful medico on his return after a longish absence; "the miltary registrar says there's a convoy of stretcher cases passing through by ambulance train to Turnberry in Ayrshire at 9 p.m. He wants me to give you a quarter of morphia and have you down at the R.T.O.'s office by then and he'll embark you as a recumbent case; he's phoning Turnberry to arrange onward transport for you to Yorkhill. It's the best way," the earnest young man went on; "you'll be under observation all the time."

I had been steeling myself not to show undue jubilation as his message percolated through to my wits but my resolve was out of place. All private wars forgotten in the face of such kindness the tears came streaming down my cheeks and I could utter no word for the great gulps that kept wracking my chest.

The doctor turned away quickly to lift a syringe and the Staff-Nurse's own eyes were moist as I held her two hands.

CHAPTER VII

Action in the "Backs to the Wall" defence of Amiens saw the last of my days as a fighting soldier. I was invalided out as a war-weary veteran at the age of twenty with three wound stripes on my sleeve. I knew by the time of my discharge that, my life having been so miraculously spared, it must now be given to tending the hurts of others; I felt I could bring understanding to the task: I was undoubtedly influenced by the fine example of the many Regimental Medical Officers I had met.

I resumed my studies as a second-year medical student at Glasgow University.

Along with other returned service men I certainly applied myself diligently to classes — we all yearned avidly to rid ourselves of the shackles of apprenticeship and to pass to the greater world of career building.

Many names now become distinguished emerged from that era of intensive post-war reaction — The late James Learmonth, Emeritus Professor Sir James, K.C.V.O., the "King's Surgeon"; John Stirling Young, M.C., Regius Professor of Pathology at Aberdeen University; John C. M. Matheson, C.B.E., D.S.O., ("Ginger") minus a limb, Senior Officer of H.M.'s Prison Medical Service; A. J. Cronin, temporary Surgeon-Probationer on destroyers; he, in "The Citadel," stormed the redoubt of Harley Street skulduggery (with his tongue in his cheek!); Tom Burton, M.C., D.C.M., one-time fellow rugger player with me, but now one-limbed, and subsequently attaining professional eminence in distant Shanghai. Walter Jope, M.C., leading figure in the Scottish Medico-political scene.

These were but some; many, many more amongst my closest friends who had answered the starter's gun with me never crossed the finishing line. Their names are enthroned within the tranquil beauty of the Shrine of Remembrance in Scotia's capital — Edinburgh Castle.

By telescoping the five-year course into four I managed to graduate in 1922 and was awarded Distinction in Medical Jurisprudence and Public Health. My first appointment took me to St. Helens in Lancashire; I became a House Surgeon in the Special Hospital, sponsored by Pilkingtons, the famous glass manufacturers. In this institution, which had as its senior consulting surgeon, the celebrated Sir Robert Jones, "Father of Orthopaedic Surgery," we dealt with all emergencies in the glass producing factories, and some indeed were fearsome; immense sheets of glass, being lifted by "sucker" attachments, frequently fell and caused devastating lacerations on the workers underneath.

In addition we housed some hundred disabled war pensioners by an arrangement with the Ministry of Pensions. Even in these early days I first made acquaintance with the expression, "Rehabilitation." Sir Robert inculcated into us junior surgeons the vital importance of re-educating crippled pensioners into capability of livelihood earning. There was a large gymnasium with all manner of ingenious remedial apparatus. There was even a school master's room where one-armed men were taught to write by a system of "mirror" caligraphy.

The resident staff, under the immediate charge of James R. Kerr, C.B.E., Ch.M. (founder President of the Association of Industrial Medical Officers) were cosmopolitan — an Englishman, a Welshman, an Irishman, an American and I, the youngest, a Scotsman! We lived together in the greatest of harmony. We even ran a horse-betting pool, to which each contributed weekly; the Englishman — a Liverpudlian — performed all the placing of money; our first bet, under his guidance, won at seven to one — a horse called Sergeant Murphy in the Grand National of that year. Unhappily subsequent gains were never realised because our Cicerone had used a Scotch bookmaker and he duly welshed!

Apart from this lighter side of life I absorbed a great deal of surgical lore from these men, all of whom became eminent; in particular, Vivian Emrys Jones became an international figure in the realms of tuberculosis; he became the titular head of the King Edward VII Memorial Tuberculosis Service of the Principality. My vicarious glory from this illustrious association, was that I became godfather to his son after his union with the Theatre Staff Nurse!

Herein, by this employment, were born in me the first seeds of what latterly became a burning desire—to establish a Rehabilitation Centre in Shetland.

In this context I must pay tribute to the two widely differing groups of doctors from whom I was to learn much; the men with whom I associated in St. Helens and the General Practitioners I was later to work with in Shetland. From both sets of medical men I acknowledge freely I learned much of human kindness no less than of practical medicine. In Lerwick alone, where the Gilbert Bain Hospital could not have functioned but for local medical co-operation, I repeated the admiration I held in Pilkington's Special Hospital for the conscientious approach and unremitting care of sick persons.

From St. Helens, on invitation, I joined the Professorial Unit in the Royal Infirmary, Glasgow; under yet another Robert, Professor Robert Kennedy.

From then on my progress, after demonstratership in the Anatomical Department of Glasgow University, was moulded in the same pattern of aspiring young surgeons in the bad old days of the Voluntary Hospitals.

I do feel impelled to record, however, that I detested the economics of the Nursing Home system of treating private patients, a system on which we all had to depend to make a living.

Although it may be that I was in danger of becoming one of Glasgow's younger breed of "fashionable" surgeons it is a fact that when the opportunity, after war's end, to become part of the Highlands and Islands Medical Service in Shetland's stimulating climate arose, it was welcomed by me, and I then resigned from the Glasgow Royal Infirmary and from the other hospital appointments I held; I had been granted indefinite leave during the national emergency; despite pressure from the Royal Infirmary to return, I opted for Shetland.

PART II

1914 - 1918 — Captain D. Lamont, Household Brigade of Artillery, under command of Colonel the Hon. John Jacob Astor (later to become Lord Astor of Hever.)

The Author, with the insignia of Brigadier, British Red Cross.

Gilbert Bain Hospital staff and associated Service personnel, 1939 - 1945. (The dog is "Winston")

A Norwegian Navy M.T.B. on patrol in the North Sea in 1944.
(Photo by courtesy of Norwegian Government)

A patient being landed from Lerwick lifeboat for transfer to an air ambulance when roads to the airport were blocked by the 1947 snow.

CHAPTER VIII

The chain of events which eventually led my hesitant foot-steps or, rather, I should say, my faltering deck-pacings, to the far-flung, northernmost islands of Great Britain, in Hitler's War, really began some twelve years earlier than the onset of that holocaust.

Fifteen years after the granting of my original Royal Artillery commission I applied to be re-animated from Reserve into the newly re-constructed Territorial Army but this time, for my *milieu*, I sought the Royal Army Medical Corps.

My motive was thus to prepare myself for the application of the quiet art of healing purpose in the war which I felt was bound, sooner or later, to rear its ugly head.

The transfer was readily effected and I was attached as second in command to Colonel Joseph A. Bingham, O.B.E., T.D., F.R.C.S., in a specialised cadre unit of my new Corps, in the 52nd (Lowland) Division under its General Officer Commanding, Major-General Sir Walter Maxwell-Scott, Bart., C.B., D.S.O., of Abbottsford, great grand-son of novelist Sir Walter Scott.

This association with Maxwell-Scott, who frequently enter--tained his officers at Abbotsford, was later on to prove the instrument for fulfilment of an ardent project of mine to bring to faraway Shetland-at-war a branch of the British Red Cross Society. My former Divisional Commander and at all times sympathetic audience to my repeated pleadings for this concession was by then retired from the Active List but had undertaken the chairmanship of the War Executive Committee of the Scottish Branch, B.R.C.S. Another helpful feature was that he had serving with him in this work, my chief and greatly respected friend in the Royal Infirmary, Lieutenant-Colonel George H. Stevenson, C.B.E., M.C., F.R.C.S., as chairman of a planning sub-committee.

With him I had already had many years association in a Red Cross enterprise, the West of Scotland Orthopaedic and Rheumatic Clinic, situated just opposite to the Scottish B.R.C.S. Headquarters in Bath Street, Glasgow.

There it was, too, I renewed my acquaintanceship with Lord Kinnaird of Rossie, chairman of the Scottish Council; not only had I known him as a squadron captain in the Scottish Horse but he had been, in 1936, Lord High Commissioner to the Church of Scotland when my Uncle Dan was Moderator of the General Assembly. My family, too, being of Argyllshire, were friends with Lady Kinnaird's people, the Talbot Cliftons of Kildalton Castle, Islay.

From him I was to learn that it had so happened that, long before my advent into Shetland, a certain military *soi disant* emissary of the Red Cross had visited the islands and an unhappy outcome, which had reflected adversely on the people, had been the result. Even the Society's President at that time, Her Majesty the Queen Mother of today, was reputed to have received an erroneous impression of the truly representative attitude of Shetland, claimed, as it was, by some to be already well enough equipped with kindred beneficent organisations.

Be that as it may, on an occasion much later on, when I had the honour of being presented to Her Majesty, in the Palace of Holyroodhouse, when some Distinguished War Service Certificates were being awarded, so apposite a remark was passed to me by Her Majesty that I realised instantly that the Royal President took more than a formal interest in Red Cross affairs, even in the remotest county branch.

That particular presentation ceremony lives on in my memory for quite another reason; it was the sole occasion when I ever had a strictly private audience of a reigning monarch — purely by a fortuitous happening or, rather, I should say now, by sheer good luck!

There were some twenty of us assembled in the Throne Room awaiting the Royal entry. Lord Kinnaird was marshalling us into line when, to my utter consternation, I found myself to be the only one carrying a cap; I was in Red Cross uniform for the occasion. Agitatedly, I asked Lord Kinnaird if there was anywhere I could plank the offending headgear but he assured me I had plenty of time to nip downstairs and deposit it in the cloakroom.

I lost no time in darting below and along the various corridors of the perfect warren which constitutes Holyroodhouse.

The cloakroom was found eventually but the return journey, in my mounting panic, was not so easy. One of the Palace Constables told me I could find a good short cut back to the Throne Room, up a winding, stone stair-case which he indicated to me. Up this spiral I shot and on rounding the last circuit came face to face with Her Majesty smilingly preparing to make her entrance through a green baize door!

Rooted to the stone steps I had just the presence of mind to murmur; "I beg your pardon, Ma'am, but I'm lost." I confess, too, that I was dazzled by the sheer beauty of Queen Elizabeth's features, when confronted at close quarters. "You can go right through;"

Her Majesty answered and gestured to the door with her gloved hand.

Through this I crept, shamefacedly and terrified, to meet the entire assembly, whose gaze was directed towards the eagerly expected Royal entry.

Later when the formal presentation was made by Lord Kinnaird, Her Majesty, with her lovely lips parted in a smile, said to me: "You have had a long journey here."

The twinkle of the eyes conveyed to me that the word "Zetland" alongside the Brigadier's insignia on my shoulder straps was not solely responsible for the remark and my face became as red as the gorgets on my lapels!

Later on, at Rossie Priory, I learned that I was indeed right in concluding that our Scottish-born Queen was deeply interested in all aspects of the Red Cross movement in her native land. I was told that every war-time County President who held her warrant of appointment was regarded by Her Majesty as being her own Red Cross representative in each area and that a personal Royal communication would be forthcoming.

This I duly received and treasure highly to this day, particularly as I was the only male person to hold such an office, with the possible exceptions of certain Lords Lieutenant and Prince Konoya of Japan!

The opposition to the founding of a Red Cross branch, voiced in some Shetlandic quarters, apart altogether from the *bêtise* of the supererogatory approach in the beginning, was based on a genuine unawareness of the world-wide implications of the Society's endeavour and its multifarious functions in time of war.

Much painstaking ante-natal manoeuvring was needed before the struggling babe of a Shetland branch could be delivered.

The decisive moment that was to ensure a successful *accouchement* took place in the Matron's room of the Gilbert Bain Memorial Hospital, the most northerly situated institution of its kind in the United Kingdom: it was at this exploratory meeting that the decision to invite people to undertake office was made and this was implemented by Maxwell-Scott. The General, although even then an ailing man, had undertaken the somewhat rigorous war-time journey northwards to lend the benefit of his knowledge and prestige. He had been invited to attend in person because I was well aware that in any insular community there is an understandable and warranted reluctance to acquiesce readily in any new ideas that are not conceived within its womb.

The stalwarts who turned the scales in the unborn infant's favour on that day were two men, both gallant veterans of World War One, the Sheriff-Substitute, R. J. Wallace, M.A., and the County Convener, Major Ted Adie, M.C.

These men, both Deputy-Lieutenants, possessed, either of them in his different way, impulses of great humaneness combined with vision and, of significant importance to my project, both were in high esteem with all those we sought to win over. They were also cognizant of all conflicting local interests which were, of course, to me, a newcomer, quite a closed book.

From my own profession I could look for little interest because, with one exception only, and he in a remote district, none had knowledge at first hand of war's hideousness nor of the assuaging boon of the multiple services to prisoners of war, the Searchers for the Missing bureau, in its war-combination with St. John's Ambulance nor the watch-dog safeguards of the International Red Cross Committee.

All the more frustrating was it, then, at our Gilbert Bain meeting, when a representative of the legal profession, invited because he held a Council appointment in the county, made this astonishing contribution to the deliberations, after hearing Sir Walter:

"I can't see that the Red Cross is wanted here; the Ladies' Guild should be able to knit any socks that may be needed."

Shades of Henri Dunant and the Geneva Convention!

Despite such obstructive pusillanimity, however, the delicate obstetrical operation was concluded and when, at last, the puling babe, delivered in much pain, was crying out for cosseting there was no lack of nutriment forthcoming from the maternal breast of the islands themselves. The person mentioned, as it happened, responded loyally.

Be it acknowledged, too, that kindly help came from afar off counties: Argyllshire, Stirlingshire, Buteshire and Roxburghshire were but some of the sources where friendly County Presidents had especial interest in hospital amenities and Shetland's Gilbert Bain happened to have particular liaison with these areas in the matter of War-time Emergency Hospitals.

No individual decorations were bestowed for Red Cross activities in Shetland-at-War but this warranted no repining for the Society is essentially a co-operative body and assumption of the "L'Etat c'est moi" mentality has no place in the cosmos of La Croix Rouge; the very soul of the work is that the doing of it should be its complete reward and there is no greater honour than the wearing of its emblem.

All unknown to me, at the time, I was, in pre-war days, forming other associations which were to have a bearing, however remote, on my Shetland transit.

Most of the time, in my Royal Infirmary appointment, I was concentrating my attention on the surgery of trauma; the casualty department was my venue for grappling with the problem of forlorn hopes and, on Receiving Nights, abundance of chestnuts were there to hand to be pulled out of the fire!

The prevailing use of whole blood for transfusion in the treatment of shock in the injured did not entirely satisfy my conception of the appropriate weapon to be used in combat against this killer. I turned to alternative synthetic fluids and was early experimenting with substitutes and colloid osmotic pressures; the gelatin in salt-solution of Hogan, the gum-salt-solution of Bayliss — I tried them all and, rather surreptitiously at times, I fear, added my own empirical ingredients!

Nowadays, of course, we have stable, effective solutions, notably Dextran, most ably investigated and standardised in Birmingham's enlightened University by such giants as John K. Squire and J. P. Bull.

Brilliant as I acknowledged their work to be I must, in loyalty to Glasgow Royal Infirmary, emphasise that it was this institution which spawned the genius who was to make Dextran's mass production a reality today.

It was the Royal's most luminous star, Joseph Lister, in association with Louis Pasteur, when working on, of all things, the fermentation of glorious beer, who noticed masses of slime impeding the purification of sugar in the refineries they visited in the course of their studies.

In 1861 they deduced that the slime was caused by Pasteur's microbes and, be it noted, these are the obliging little agents employed in the manufacture of Dextran in 1957.

Mention of Joseph Lister recalls to me a privilege once accorded to me and of which, as a worshipper of his, I am extremely proud.

I feel sure that my one-time charge and friend would take no offence when I interpolate here that I was enabled on an occasion to render a service to this man who not only bore the Master's name but was intimately associated with his private life.

He was the son of Lord Lister's Edinburgh assistant, Sir William Watson Cheyne, Bart., K.C.M.G., F.R.S. (Sir William Macewan having been his Glasgow counterpart) for Lister was impelled to emigrate to the capital following on disagreement with the Royal's managers, an issue brought to climax by his wasting of time in the unorthodox behaviour of spraying carbolic acid solution all about the place!

The son was Colonel Sir Joseph Lister Cheyne, Bart, M.C., (and bar), late Commanding Officer, 16/5th Lancers. He had a home in Shetland's north-easterly island of Fetlar, which I have often visited; there in a beautiful sea-girt setting stands the mansion with a rose-garlanded *piazza* of glass, the pride of its creator's artistry and in it the father wrote his monumental book on tuberculosis of bones and joints.

Lord Lister's wedding gift to his assistant reposes in the home of its present owner in Lerwick; it is a thing of rare beauty, a bedroom suite in mellow rose-wood. The fortunate possessor, also a friend of mine, has, on occasion, been kind enough to let me devour its loveliness with my eyes.

But these acquisitive organs are all that have been permitted to acquire anything of it! Should she ever chance to notice this let it be observed that I am still anything but sales-resistant should she so care!

When I look back to the time when the old Lister Block in the Royal was demolished, in the interests of space clearance in the quadrangle, and the people journeyed from far and near, from America, Australia and even from Japan just to secure some little wooden trophy, constructed from the benches in Lister's lecture theatre, I know that I might conceivably meet with some slight opposition at any auction in Lerwick!

Respite from the toil of Royal Infirmary days was gained by attendance at the annual Territorial camp. With my friend and partner in many a convivial ploy, Joe Bingham, we were brigaded on alternate years with the Highland Light Infantry and those staunch Covenanters, The Cameronians.

Many splendid days were spent on the sea-lapped sand dunes of Ayrshire. Gailes Camp, adjacent to such golfers' paradises as Troon and Old Prestwick, of which we were made honorary members, lives on in memory of gladsome days of sunshine, horse-riding and fine camaraderie.

With the lapse of some three years Joe, his tour in command now ended, passed to one of the Cameronian Battalions as Regimental M.O., with Colonel Sir Douglas McKinnes Shaw, D.S.O., as commanding officer.

In this officers' mess, now Joe's successor at Yorkhill, I was ever sure of a welcome both from him and from his C.O., a fine upright and gifted Deputy in Glasgow's Lieutenancy. It was through this association too that I first made the acquaintance of one who was to figure prominently in my going to Shetland. This was the Commanding Officer of the 6th Battalion, The Cameronians, the Right Honourable David John Colville, M.P., H.M. Secretary of State for Scotland and, later, the first Baron Clydesmuir.

A former Member of Parliament himself, tall, handsome Douglas McKinnes Shaw and I, his very antithesis, formed a bond of friendship forged in a common love of championing, in our different spheres, the apparently lost cause.

He it was who assailed the impregnable fortress of redoubtable

Jimmy Maxton in the Bridgeton division and even if he did not gain the seat he made an appreciable dent in it!

Had events transpired otherwise he could have been, as was indeed mooted at the time, the one to have given the present mission-inspired and personable leader of the Liberal Party, Jo Grimond, the sort of contest of which he is worthy in the Orkney and Shetland parliamentary division when beloved Sir Basil Neven-Spence retired after his fifteen years of unstinted service, both as Member and as invaluable Committeeman.

Unhappily, *dis aliter visum* for Douglas was but another of those who has but recently paid the last toll of all to the scarified bridges which he crossed as the youngest colonel in the British Army, over the battlefields of Flanders in the earlier Armageddon.

He was, however, to be my guest repeatedly in Shetland for his ardent patriotism and duty-sense brought him back again into the arena, this time, as chance decreed it, to the defences of the northerly Atlantic islands for a while.

His responsibility was to be the deployment and construction of the anti-aircraft gun-sites in the Shetland group, amongst others, wherein rested the security of Scapa Flow as a naval base.

His headquarters he made further south and he visited Shetland only from time to time as he quite frankly confessed that the war-time atmosphere of Lerwick held no appeal for him. He did not like what he termed the "false urbanity" of that town's optimates, with whom he had dealings.

I can well understand this reaction in a man with such out-standing candour in his make-up for the stranger within its waters, or "South-mouther" as the local idiom has it, either decides to accept, albeit with reservations of his own, the façade of forthrightness offered to him by Lerwick and to love the place or he just can't abide it and detests it.

There is no middle road for even the most lyrical admirer of the little town, and I count myself as one, cannot evade the evidence that your Lerwegian has never yet learned to laugh at himself, what though he can do so right heartily at others and criticism from outwith the circle of his own kind is anathema to him.

It must always be remembered too that Lerwick has its hinter-land, including the outlying islands, whence springs the true aristocracy of Shetland, the tillers of the soil and the men whose calling is the sea.

When Jo Grimond contested the seat not only did he bring his great natural gifts to the platform but he showed a ready adapta-bility to the way of life of the islanders. I have seen him land from a small craft on westerly Burra Isle, stroll bare-headed past the knot of blue-guernseyed fishermen at the pier-head and advance to the net-festooned poles further up the rough road-track. There, quite casually, but with practised eye and fingers, would he conduct a search for the destructive rents from voracious dog-fish. Then he would make his way, still in quite leisurely fashion, to the little hall to give his address, which would be completely redolent of knowledge in regard to local affairs.

Not so his ill-fated opponent, Mr Archibald Tennant, the scion of many noble families and a man reared in the midst of politics — as known in Whitehall and the Central Office of the Conservative Party!

Of such fine integrity was poor Archie Tennant that I have heard him answer a questioner on some matter of local economy; "I really don't know."

Surely a unique reply in the annals of the hustings!

He would have done better to have taken a leaf out of the book of the Right Honourable Walter Elliott, C.H., M.C., M.P., who came up to support him.

Whenever Walter received a facer on matters on which he chanced to be a little less well informed than Encyclopaedia Britannica he made instant riposte, with chapter and verse, of some extremely apt Biblical quotation.

I confess that assiduous search later through the Book of Leviticus failed to confirm his authoritative explanation as to why Pharaoh hanged the baker!

The islands, of course, are traditionally Liberal in their political outlook and Sir Basil Neven-Spence's wresting of the seat from that persuasion was a monumental feat.

Once he retired the natural reaction of the people was to revert to their forefather's trend and therein again Jo had a decided advantage.

He had also, and I repeat that this was in addition to his own personal talent and flair, the asset of the support in the being of his mother-in-law, Lady Violet Bonham Carter, who was known to be held in high regard by Sir Winston Churchill.

When Lady Violet was making a proselytizing tour she came to Lerwick and my wife and I were happy to offer her some slight hospitality and rest-time in our home.

At the risk of betraying the sacred trust of a host I cannot resist a sly dig, even at the ranks of Tuscany!

Lady Violet had been discoursing in our lounge on the subject of the essential need for a Liberal Government to arrest the mounting cost of living.

She spoke earnestly and eloquently on the burden placed on the housewife of a limited budget so I asked her what was the current price of bacon.

The reply was like Archie Tennant's: "I'm afraid I don't know at the moment!"

Let there be, however, no misunderstanding of my sentiments; along with the vast majority of thinking people I know that the islanders, both Orcadian and Shetlandic, are well served by Jo Grimond.

The peculiar individual characteristics of the Shetland Island group, brought about by its archipelago formation, can only be harmonised by a man of outstanding personality and integrity and in the political sphere their member fulfils these desiderata.

In the local scene it has always seemed to me that Sir Basil Neven-Spence epitomises everything that is finest in the Shetland Islander.

I have seen him one week with his sleeves rolled up, building a road on the island of Uyea, which he owns, and doing so with expertise. I have seen him the following week in the livery of the Royal Company of Archers, the Queen's personal bodyguard in Scotland.

A typical Shetlander he can do anything, he can go anywhere!

It was an auspicious thing for the islands that some years ago the decision to create a Lieutenancy quite separate from that of Orkney was made and the Sovereign's representative inevitably came to be Sir Basil, ensconced, as he is, in the true udalling traditions of his birth-land and in his authoritative knowledge of the fishing industry.

For any self-hypnotised pocket Hercules coming in through the South-mouth, to foster a smoky pipe-dream, soused down perhaps by subterranean waterways, of diverting the Lieutenant's Letters Patent from Sir Basil, would have been indeed a futile thirteenth labour, akin to a pompous little firkin's trying to assume the stature of more than half a kilderkin! One such did try — abortively — I happen to know.

CHAPTER IX

For many years along with the absorption in trauma the study and treatment of cancer claimed my interest. This had its inspiration in an invitation extended to me by Sir George T. Beatson, K.C.B., K.B.E., to come on as his assistant in the Glasgow Royal Cancer Hospital and the associated West of Scotland Radium Institute, the whole beautifully equipped building being now re-named the Royal Beatson Hospital in honour of its founder.

Today this institution figures prominently in the research crusade against the solacing cigarette as a malign genius in the lungs. The Director of Research, my friend and quondum colleague, Philip R. Peacock, has a most diverting *sabotage* of doves all assiduously trained to puff away continually at the fragrant weed through an assembly of glass tubes and I must say *they* seem to like it!

In my day the sacrificial altar lodged the domestic fowl and inoffensive little white mice which were given cutaneous inunction with dibenzanthracene-lard or, more succintly, plain tar on the scruff of the neck!

Sir George Beatson's offer was the more acceptable to me just then as, to my chagrin I had recently failed to secure an appointment which I had coveted in the Royal, the post of genito-urinary surgeon in a newly created department in that specialty.

The appointment went to one whose artistry in the operating theatre is admittedly a joy to watch and he a close friend and lovable soul withal.

Be that as it may when the death of Sir George sadly put an end to our amiable relationship and I succeeded to his wards I was given the gracious pleasure of bestowing largesse on the same successful rival! The *amende honorable* was effected by his humbly craving a few beds in my side-rooms to follow the pursuit of his fell cystoscopic purposes!

It must in fairness be conceded that the patients benefited immensely by his recruitment and if ever such intimate affairs as are embraced within his speciality should go wrong in my aging anatomy then my man is Mr Arthur Henry Jacobs, President-Emeritus, Urological Section, Royal Society of Medicine.

One of the happiest recollections of those days is my association with Sally T——, more decorously styled, Miss Cicely Turner, R.R.C., then the Sister in Charge but later to be Matron. Beloved by every-one (especially me!) she was to have a most amazing and distinguished war career which ranged from Cruden Bay in Scotland to Abyssinia and the East with whistle-stops in France, Tunisia and Malta.

At one time before Dunkirk, Sally, the last to leave the remnant of her hospital, dashed down the road simultaneously hold-ing up her dainty furbelows and the advancing Germans what time she gave them a right good lashing with her honest Pitlochry tongue!

She was the finest Nurse I ever knew.

Arising out of this fresh interest in malignant disease and sponsored by the National Radium Commission I travelled to London to make special study of techniques practised by two acknowledged leaders of my choice.

The first to receive me which he did with infinite kindness was Sir Stanford Cade, K.B.E., C.B., F.R.C.S., now Senior Surgeon, Westminster Hospital. In war time he became Consultant in Surgery to the Royal Air Force with the temporary rank of Air Vice-Marshal.

My especial interest at the time was in malignant disease of the breast and it was a curious thing that the other man to welcome me generously in London, Sir Geoffrey Langdon Keynes, Saint Bartholomew's Hospital and Radium Institute, Mount Vernon, pos-sessing diametrically opposite views to Cade, yet came to hold the same rank as Senior Consultant to the Royal Air Force and in this capacity I was to meet him in Shetland.

From Keynes I heard nothing but eulogy of the method by which radium needles are embedded in a sort of cuirasse of dental composition and the whole applied to the sufferer's body.

Cade was vehement that the needles must be brought to closest apposition with the growth by direct implantation into and around the breast tissue.

I came down heavily on the side of Cade's method; quite possibly I was influenced by its protagonist's being such an admirable host in his Harley Street home!

But Geoffrey Keynes apparently bore no ill-will on this score for after he had visited me once or twice in war-time Shetland, clad in the habiliments of his exalted rank, he wrote to me à propos a project then on foot. This was the contemplated formation of a separate Royal Air Force hospital within the islands, designed for the exclusive care of the personnel belonging to Coastal, Fighter and Bomber Command then all operating from there.

The gist of the letter was generous like the man; it indicated that the decision reached, on his advice, was that the care of these flying men already rested safely in the existing emergency hospital arrangements.

From then onwards the R.A.F. sick-quarters establishments

and myself worked together in utter cordiality.

With these varying professional interests the years slipped on towards the fateful moment in 1939.

Additional other appointments had come my way and chill penury, for long a Jeremiah-like familiar, took its very acceptable congé!

With it all the lure of trauma held its supreme fascination. The enlightenment that well became the managers of an institution which had nurtured Joseph Lister was made manifest by their removing the grave responsibility of the casualty department from the puling babes of the profession.

It was early realised, although it has taken longer for England so to do, that this department is the display window of any hospital and depending on the quality of service rendered there, will the grievously injured patient survive or the reverse be the case; so must the extent of a hospital's usefulness to the community be judged.

The special reconstructive skills of the surgeons, be they plastic, orthopaedic, general or ophthalmic can never reach the patient if the initial measures of resuscitation to save his life are not promptly applied the very moment the so-called irreversibly shocked patient crosses the threshold.

The favourable reversibility of the injured one's state can be achieved only by affording him immediately and on the spot the special skills of seasoned experience in this field.

Such places as Cardiff Royal Infirmary, Birmingham's famed Accident Hospital and Rehabilitation Centre with some few others have long since proved it.

For myself, continually pondering over the problem of resuscitation, the test was soon to come as it was for a startled nation.

A slight breathing space was afforded following the blast from the warning herald in 1938 when the infamous agreement between Britain, France, Germany and Italy, in respect of Sudetenland in Czecho-Slovakia, was made.

Munich!

I was not called upon to mobilise for, some time previously, I had requested re-transfer back to Reserve as the demands of consulting practice left little time for anything but sleep and even this had often to be covertly snatched pari passu with the reading of innumerable scientific journals!

The decision, I am sure, was a wise one on another count, an aspect voiced to me by the Director of Hygiene in the War Office, Major-General John Alexander Manifold, C.B., D.S.O., a distinguished pathologist, a King's Household Physician who was to become Deputy Director of Medical Services to Scottish Command in 1941 and always, for me, a great stalwart of strength and support in occasional diversity of views with brigadiers in Shetland as to the proper functions of civil hospitals.

Prior to that, referring to the utilisation of medical man-power in war, he had said to me; "We shall want all the experts in orthopaedic and traumatic surgery doing their own job when it comes; the mistake last time was to put you people into high-ranking administrative posts and, as I have known it, even into Regimental Aid Posts."

Proof of the folly he was indicating was early forthcoming when, with war finally upon us, probably Edinburgh's most gifted and promising of the younger surgeons, Colonel Stewart Middleton ("Sam") tragically lost his life in one of those all-too-common transport air crashes. A highly popular and enthusiastic Territorial officer in Edinburgh's Field Ambulance he was moving merely to some trifling administrative affair in his new capacity as a Divisional Assistant Director of Medical Servces.

Instead of being faced with the dismal prospect of finding myself tied to a martial desk I was asked to specify the capacity in which the Central Medical War Committee could ear-mark me for consulting surgical employment.

I endorsed my letter: "Anywhere, home or abroad. Would like Royal Navy for a change."

This request, much later, was to provide me with my greatest personal problem in Shetland.

As it was, when the ultimatum from Chamberlain finally burst upon the world I had much to do in preparation for the call I expected hourly. Decidedly I had no inkling of what was to await me in Latitude 60° N.

*   *   *   *   *

Following on the vital final declaration there were to be hectic days of evacuation of the patients from the various hospitals in which I held appointments, straining nights of picking one's way through the black-out to operate, panic appeals to colleagues to take over private patients in nursing homes, rush arrangements with accountants and bankers, doleful nights with public houses closing at eight p.m.!

But as regards the Royal Navy — not a sausage save an eager, matutinal scrutiny of the mail!

I did have, in fact, some active war employment during the first month; I had been made Director of a Mobile Surgical Unit and, although my heart was not in it, I set about recruiting as likely a looking team as I could find, a registrar, physicians, anaesthetists, blood-transfusionists and so on.

Then, quite unexpectedly, Sir Douglas McKinnes Shaw came to me. He was at the time on the staff-nucleus of General Le Fanu and was engaged in assembling a Divisional Headquarters of a Scottish formation that was to become famous, the 15th Division.

Feeling sure that my naval aspirations had been docketed and forgotten I agreed to go on with General Le Fanu as A.D.M.S., with the rank of full Colonel which the appointment carried.

Even before my tailor had completed the necessary augmentations to my tunic I received another summons of a different calibre altogether. It came with the compliments of the Chief Medical Officer of the Department of Health for Scotland, then Doctor Macintosh. Could I name a time when it would be convenient to meet his representative at the Department's office in Glasgow on a matter of urgency?

I could.

The question put to me was whether I would be willing to go to the Shetland Isles in a temporary capacity as consulting surgeon.

It appeared that the incumbent of the post of Surgeon-Consultant, as was the designation used in the Highlands and Islands Medical Service, had flown away in response to an R.A.F.V.R. commitment whilst a holiday *locum tenens* was in his place.

It was further indicated to me that there was some difficulty with the Navy on the latter score but the nature of this was then unspecified although subsequently it was to be boomed out to me in Shetland with a vengeance, I must say!

"Will you go there if only to hold the fort until someone is appointed?" The C.M.O.'s emissary wanted to know.

I told him I had already fixed up to go off with Army Medical Services but he pressed his suit by declaring; "Leave all that to us, Mr Lamont. Any difficulty with the War Office will just cause a little pressure to be brought to bear."

I replied that I was not worried about the War House but that I could not go back on my word to Colonel McKinnes Shaw and that before any decision was made I must see him. Without prejudice, all the same, I wanted to know what sort of work the job in Shetland entailed.

All was delightfully vague as, indeed, it continued to be along the entire line.

"I don't really know except that war casualties are expected and everybody, including the Minister himself, thinks you're the very man for this particular task;" was the civil servant's answer and he added; "The C.M.O. wants you to leave within twenty-four hours, though. Can you do that?"

"Only if Colonel Shaw releases me and you fix things with the Royal Infirmary.

"Anyhow, how would I get there?"

He didn't know.

I sought out Douglas at his office in Park Circus and although put out at having his arrangements upset he was entirely accommodating.

"It's very evident they want you, Dan;" he encouraged; "and I think you should go. You will be right in the thick of it up there and you'll get all the wounded you'll want from the sea if not the air."

His words were to prove accurately prophetic.

A special meeting of the Royal's House Committee was convened that afternoon and I was granted leave of absence for the period of national emergency by the Managers.

They wished me good fortune and looked forward to my speedy return then added this priceless gem of advice which I should have been all the better to have heeded.

"Be sure you have a firm contract with these Department of Health people as to your emoluments before ever you set off."

Those words were to prove equally as clairvoyant as Douglas Shaw's for in all the rush of my departure no one saw fit to mention what in modern parlance would be called the "lolly" and it was some three months later before they started to hand it out! An interesting point emerges here, also, for I found that the Naval Base, having control of their own local finance, paid me in hard cash for individual items of service but the Army limited their advances to the presentation of forms in triplicate! The Air Force blithely ignored the whole question and nobody cared much either way!

On that same night of my acceptance of the interim mandate I dined with the Secretary of State in the Conservative Club and received an informal briefing.

The purport of Colonel Colville's conversation, if a little nebulous, was at least informative by reason of what it failed to specify in many directions.

"No need to point out to an old campaigner like yourself the importance that the Atlantic islands must assume in time of war, especially as we can expect submarine attack in excess of the last show's.

"You will too, I think, appreciate the importance of the Shetlands when I tell you that Scapa Flow in the Orkneys, a hundred miles further south will likely be the last remaining base for the Home Fleet.

"Irish ports are by no means certain; the Mersey's unsuitable and the Clyde yards are likely to be busy in other directions."

He must even then, I was to see in retrospect, have been envisaging the transatlantic interchange of traffic and transports which indeed was later to emerge under Lease-Lend agreement but, of course, he could not have known it as that.

South coast anchorages and dockyards obviously were to be vulnerable to constant harassment and interruption from the air but the reference to Irish ports was obscure at the time.

The matter was illuminated by Churchill's own words, quoted in the Press, when, with submarine sinkings steadily gaining momentum, he paid his memorable tornado-like visit to Scapa following the torpedoing of the *Royal Oak* within the Flow and set on foot the building of the inter-island causeways, there to the present day, a boon to all Orcadian transport.

His words were to the effect that an insufferable burden was being placed upon the nation by the denial of Irish ports for our ships by Eire's shameful assumption of neutrality.

When I heard these words I recalled the S.O.S.'s statement in the Conservative Club.

At that time, too, Colonel Colville added another significant remark which tells me now that much more prescience existed in Chamberlain's Government than for which ever I, for one, gave it credit.

I should say that the First Lord of the Admiralty was the genius of vision whom the Secretary was again quoting to me.

"The Shetlands, at the extreme north, would provide an ideal turning point for the enemy, if he managed to seize a corresponding base in the very south.

"With these new long-range Condors he's got he could not only neutralise Scapa but he could have a to and fro service to bomb the entire country without having to return to Germany to refuel."

I thought long over this. It seemed to me that it was envisaged that the Channel Islands would be attacked either simultaneously or prior to Shetland and not myself being then fully alive to the possibilities of an airborne supply line, I concluded that the European coast must be reached by the enemy as a first measure. This I decided could only be achieved by a complacent Spain and a subjugated Portugal.

Never for the moment was the fall of France considered as an eventuality to make practicable the shuttle service adumbrated by the S.O.S. I am sure that neither of these occupations was in his mind either but I am not so certain that the fall of Denmark and Norway was out of his reckoning.

When shortly afterwards the enemy were in fact allowed to occupy Guernsey and Alderney without opposition I recalled the S.O.S.'s words and viewed the seizure with more equanimity than most; it meant, by my reasoning, that Shetland, where I was by then stationed would be defended to the utmost and that was a comfort as I very much wanted to see the Royal Infirmary again!

Interested as I was in what I had been told of the strategical situation by the S.O.S. I still wanted some information along more immediate personal lines. What was to be my status with the Armed Forces and where did civilian cases stand in the matter of priority of treatment?

Again everything was quite airy-fairy.

"Doctor Mackintosh thinks you would be best just to go as interim Surgeon-Consultant for the present; what transpires later depends entirely on how things develop, especially as we have no idea of how much bombing you will get. A great deal must be left to your discretion and you will send us an appreciation of the whole picture once you have had time to study it on the spot.

"You can rely on full backing from the Department in all your difficulties and, quite honestlyl, I think you will have a lot!"

Again, here was a true prognostication!

"The Navy is raising some sort of a moan over the present arrangements for surgical emergencies; that's why we're rushing you, a senior man, up there and each of us thinks you'll get on well with them, the Air Force too and, of course, you already know the Army inside out.

"By the way, it's an Irish surgeon named Wheeler who is advising the Naval blokes: he knows you and has spoken highly of you so they can have no further cause to grouse.

"So-long and good luck!"

That was all; no mention of what hospitals I was to serve; their size, how they were equipped or staffed or who ran them. No mention of any Board of Trustees of whose very existence I was to learn only after some time's residence in Lerwick.

They, who controlled the hospital administration, I was to find, knew as much about me as I did about them — exactly nothing!

No mention of where I was to live or even how I was to reach Shetland in time of war or who was going to pay my fare to get there!

In the event no one ever did meet that deductable expense but me! The Honorary Secretary to the Trustees told me that when one was in receipt of a substantial salary one was expected to pay one's travelling expenses and he added, helpfully, that if ever I wanted leave I would require to find and renumerate my own locum!

Truly a free-lance mission if ever there was one!

But if His Majesty's Secretary of State for Scotland, the titular head of Scotia's Department of Health, was uninformed in all these matters I knew someone immediately to my hand in that club who would not be so illiterate!

I consulted old Andrew Wilson the head waiter.

E

CHAPTER X

Fair Isle, of the Shetland group, had hitherto been to me but a slightly exotic name suggestive of some garish sort of fancy-patterned pullover people affected on the golf course.

Now Andrew was to show me on the map in the library the minute oceanic spot that was his birth-place.

"You're not going away entirely beyond the reach of civilisation; the people are really quite well educated," he assured me and judging by his own detailed knowledge of the choicer wines, *mises en bouteille au chateau,* or not so *"mised"* I was well prepared to accept the understatement; all the more especially as I had just overheard Alan Inverclyde consult his advice on the vintage port!

I learned much from Andrew; he was only too willing to wait well on into the night to assuage the thirst of an avid pilgrim to his beloved home-land. He told me a deal of Fair Isle and the shocking treatment the poor inhabitants received from a skinflint County Council with especial reference to the niggardly refusal to pay for the men's dedicated toil in transporting a windlass, which they had filched from Orkney, to the South Haven. There were, too, the terrible hardships endured by the crew of the smallest mail-boat plying the Atlantic, *The Good Shepherd.* The subsidy from the Government, it appeared, was entirely insufficient to compensate them for the travail of carrying the post-bag along with their own island stores, from Grutness on the Shetland mainland.

"They do not so badly, all the same;" he did concede eventually and I would rate this now as among the classic understatements.

Of Lerwick he had little to say; "There's not much social activity; the two hotels are a bit out of date."

I gathered that, in contrast to this, Fair Isle and westerly placed Foula, "The Edge of the World," were centres of sybaritic revelry and lush caravanserai!

"I don't have much knowledge of the Gilbert Bain Hospital; I never bothered a lot about such places but I often read about the staff being thanked in the death notices in "The Shetland Times;" was a statement not calculated to extend the field of knowledge very much.

But thus it was early on that I was to receive my first inkling that with your Shetlander an open disarming countenance does not always connote dull wits. In fact, one of these same Fair Islanders, by name Stout, came to be the Prime Minister of New Zealand.

The islanders' playful conversational habit is based on the Greek cult of *meiosis,* if not the actual perversion of the spoken word from what he means you to understand.

In the Conservative Club, in one respect of great importance to me, where Ministerial ill-appraisal obtained, Fair Isle Ganymede was instinct with up-to-date exactitude. He knew precisely how to get to Shetland even in these days when the normal air and sea facilities were completely disrupted and the movements of ships were disclosed to no one, partly in deference to Defence of the Realm requirements no doubt, but, just as cogently, because no one save the captains was in a position to know — except our Andrew from the Fair Isle!

The same island, I must add, proved to be for me an oasis of delight in its watery isolation and I came in time to love it and all who dwell therein, the Stouts, the Wilsons and the Eunsons — all the three!

Colonel Colville's reference to the Navy's surgical adviser had intrigued me. I realised he meant Sir William Ireland de Courcy Wheeler. I knew him from contact at the annual meetings of the Association of Surgeons of Great Britain and Ireland and I knew that, formerly Professor of Surgery at Trinity College, he had literally been forced to flee Dublin on account of his loyal adherence to the Crown.

I had been lucky in being given the Fellowship of the select Association at an early age without having to go through the probationary stage of Associate member. This concession was through the generous sponsorship of one of the most courtly and great-hearted surgeons it has been my good fortune to assist, Mr John Patrick, who was one of Wheeler's intimate friends and the latter had supported my election.

John Patrick originally introduced me to the Irish surgeon at a dinner in the Royal College of Surgeons and he it was who told me the story of the Dublin flight.

In the first world-war Sir William had been Lieut.-Colonel R.A.M.C. When, with peace restored, the turn of the teaching centre, Dublin, came round for the Association's three-day meeting to be held there and the Professor would naturally be taking the chair as host, he received a call from the Minister of the Interior, one named Ryan, who instructed him that the Government of Eire forbade that the English National Anthem be *played* at the customary banquet, always a quite grand affair with all "decorations to be worn" trimmings, etcetera.

On the night of the dinner Sir William, liberally festooned

with his "gongs," vociferously led the *singing* of the hymn.

The result was his enforced departure from his Chair of Surgery and from his very country where he occupied it. He came to London but, even for a surgeon who had been knighted by his King and especially for one of senior years, it proved to be a long, long time before he found employment and, as he put it himself, he was right down on his very uppers.

By the time of the second world-war the position had been retrieved and his eminence was again such that he was given appointment in the rank of Temporary Surgeon Rear-Admiral, R.N.

In this capacity he was based on the requisitioned mental hospital, Kingseat, Aberdeen, where the naval surgeons their wonders did perform.

He loved to make the passage northwards, see an odd case or two in the Naval Auxiliary Sick Quarters and then adjourn to Lerwick's Queen's Hotel where he would sleep overnight; or at least he slept part of it for the first half was invariably spent in keeping his cronies mesmerised with his sparkling wit and fund of spontaneous anecdotes.

I used to ask him to come up periodically as I loved to have him, not so much for his professional assistance, but just to listen to him.

On one of these jaunts I was assisting him to don his top-coat, heavily gilded with the bewildering regalia of his rank.

He caught me peering intently at the muster of gold on his shoulder straps. With perplexed anxiety the soldier-turned-sailor inquired in his lovely Irish brogue; "What's wrong with the bluidy things this time, Lamont?" thereby indicating there had been a former occasion to give him a guilty conscience!

"Is me Crown and Anchor board not formin' fours the proper way to be pleasin' you?"

Then he went off on a train of thought prompted by some association of ideas:

"These be wondrous days we live in, Lamont. They talk of Black Shirts; they talk of Brown Shirts and even have I heard tell of Green Shirts.

"Bedad, if just one of the divils had to walk about London without any shirt at all . . . ."

The crinkling Irish laughter and the quizzical look lent entrancing conclusion to the quip.

With it all Wheeler was ever eager to be of any assistance whatsoever in helping us to overcome difficulties.

So assiduous, indeed, was he in this that he it was who later caused me many long hours of thought in reaching a decision that

was to influence my whole career, for better or for worse I do not
even now know.

* * * * *

Four days my initial passage took from Aberdeen to Lerwick,
a furious gale raging across the Pentland Firth in the early hours
of a Sunday. There was to be for us, however, a peaceful awakening
in the sheltered reaches of Kirkwall harbour. The sun shone brightly
and the water, I remarked, crested with carnaptious little white
horses, was intensely blue.

The Roads were filled with a vast motley of foreign shipping
and during our enforced stay, I learned many things.

The nearest vessel to us wore a patchwork of multi-coloured
flags and the mendacious lettering "Republic of Panama" prominently
on her hull's top-sides.

She was a German.

Outside of her was yacht-like *St. Sunniva* known to me already
as the elegant "White Lady of the North" which was wont to pass
up in more gracious days off the Fifeshire coast as I would be golfing
at Crail. Alas, no longer her charming self she was painted Admiralty
grey and, devoid of her nobly-planned figure-head, mounted two
quite unladylike twelve pounders, fore and aft.

The tragic fate awaiting her was to be mortally crushed in
Arctic ice whilst steaming as reserve ship behind convoys, an assault
for the bearing of which her delicate scantlings were never designed.

The ships lay there, docile and quiet, flying, at the forepeak,
the blue-bordered red and white flag which gave intimation that
they awaited clearance papers from the Royal Navy following
examination by Contraband Control.

Fussy little tug-boats buzzed about and, no doubt, were diligent
in well-doing and justifying the taxpayers' contributions to demurrage
and kindred other expenses.

The naval boarding party of two officers and six ratings would
behave with laudable courtesy and, whilst apologising to a ship's
Master for the delay, unobtrusively seal the wireless cabin!

If the Ministry of Economic Warfare, following on the receipt
of a teleprint from Kirkwall, decided on further examination a Prize
Court sat and decided on the ultimate destination of the cargo and
on any compensation payable to the owners for confiscation.

One astute transatlantic shipping company, finding itself in
unprofitable possession of some unsaleable lots of derelict junk, old
pianos, decayed furniture and the like, loaded it up and deliberately
ordered their Captain into the North Sea.

They were hugely delighted that he should be deflected into
Kirkwall where the objective of the ship was declared to be Hamburg.

Slightly less jubilant was the Master when, still with unfailing politeness, he was let loose into the watery wastes with the order, "Proceed with all despatch to your port of destination, Captain!"

Of more sinister import were the craft bearing the bogus marking of "Danmark" and carrying a deck cargo of wood.

Such might be brought in because an ever-vigilant Fifth Destroyer Flotilla would not fail to observe significant alterations of the vessel's freeboard on passage. Even when apparently engaged in the innocent pursuit of commerce such a ship would always ride a foot or two higher in the water after discharge of a below-deck cargo of oil into the rapacious maw of an under-sea boat.

On the Tuesday we resumed our Odyssey which brought us past the half-way Paddy's Milestone, the Fair Isle.

My particular, joyous companion of the voyage was a retired sea captain making for his final berth in his home-port and, as we stood on the bridge, clutching the rail, *R.M.S. St. Clair* pitched rolled, thumped and bucketed. She, too, I was to know well as a theatre-equipped rescue ship behind convoys.

It must have been a full-sized gale still for even the ship's Master, a native of Argyllshire like myself, conceded that the breeze was tending to freshen again!

My own rollicking cicerone, as we entered the Roost, where Atlantic Ocean, North Sea, wind and tide were each in conflict *à outrance,* regaled me with a graphic account of how his ship, *Nolander,* had just here buried her nose in the same sort of rip and he was fortunate to be rescued!

His other enlivening tale was of a slight navigational error in 1915, in respect of this mine-swept channel, south'ard of Shetland, when there had been just one big bang and she was down!

Altogether absorbing as I found this to be, the anticipation of ever seeing the Macewan plaque in Glasgow's Royal Infirmary was receding hourly.

Captain Macmillan himself, subsequently Commodore of the Company's fleet, was a great character although his origins in Argyll were not all they should have been! He did not come from the Lamont ancestral lands in fair Cowal but from the rival clan's, the Campbells, in the Island of Tiree.

All through the war he plied up and down that turbulent course, his later command being *St. Magnus* and the decoration he received was well merited indeed.

No great lover of Lerwick, or so he professed, he spurned the oft-heard claim that the Shetlander made the finest seaman in the world.

But then Mac was a law unto himself. On one of the many passages I made with him we were escorted by an armed White Sea trawler from Hull.

As we zig-zagged down the mine-swept channel, green water coming inboard with every alteration of course, *St. Magnus* repeatedly incurred the wrath of our escort.

"Don't you dare swing away from the course I keep giving you;" flashed the trawler's Aldis at us time and again.

"Tell him to keep his hair on;" Mac ordered his bridge officer to reply and, turning to me, added: "I'll teach him to talk like that to a real sailor."

He did not see fit to relay the Navy's riposte but, unknown to Mac, I had read it off myself.

"Sorry; no can do. Would need to come on your bridge to get the necessary hair-pins."

When the Old Man's health finally broke down, doubtless the aftermath of his war service on that route, I visited him in hospital outside Edinburgh. The tears were in his eyes as he spoke of the past and shyly he slipped to me a florin, which I'm sure he could ill afford, as a gift for my little boy, who was often a passenger with me and a great favourite of the ship.

CHAPTER XI

Tuesday evening, under the flickering canopy of these merry dancers, the Northern Lights, saw our arrival alongside in the harbour of peninsular-sited Lerwick; the island of Bressay, lying like a watch-dog *couchant* off-shore, was only just discernible.

There was nobody to greet me.

Knowing nothing of the island's hospital economy I set about to find the naval officer in charge and to learn the causes of friction with the Department I represented, the telegraphic address of which is "Health."

I was fortunate to see a long, gangling and sad figure who assured me he was the Chief Constable.

No doubt actuated by spy-conscious zeal he surveyed me with considerable suspicion when I declared my objective and asked for guidance. But somewhere in my hold-all I had my current passport and that opened the sesame of caution for me.

When eventually I entered the Presence, in a little room adjacent to the residents' lounge in the Queen's Hotel, my immediate appraisal was that I faced a maritime version of Colonel Blimp. The ribbon of the Distinguished Service Order, on the chest of the Post-Captain, however, counselled reserve in that preliminary assessment.

The attendant secretary, a two and a half ringer of ingenuous, rosy countenance was addressed as "Sonny" and it all seemed too kindergarten for the serious business of waging war.

Therein was to be my first error of accepting the obvious in these islands; that same Pay Lieutenant-Commander was later to lose his life in gallant circumstances and the Senior Naval Officer, Colin Inglis, was to prove a very helpful shipmate on board the Shetland barque.

But, before all that, there were to be considerable ripplings of the surface in that little sitting-room. The exchanges were conducted with full quarter-leck *fortissimo* and, highly keyed as I was to "careless talk" I could not but wonder how the occupants of the lounge next door, let alone the ground-floor diners and even the people at the extreme top of the house, were lapping it all up!

The opening naval gambit, when I had handed over my card,

came with the bourdon stop of the organ full out·

"If you attempt to leave these islands I shall have an armed guard of marines placed on you!"

I replied meekly that I had come at the request of the Secretary of State to do a bit of operating and anyway it was a little too rough for my idea of travel.

Empurpling rather much for the good of his blood-pressure, which I was quick to point out to the virtual viceroy, he boomed at me:

"Who the hell are those 'Health' people that keep sending telegrams here? The surgeon they've left here in this base may be damned good at his own job but he's right out of his depth and he's been trying his get-away all the time."

I sprang to the defence of a colleague; "If that's so then it must be he objects to being bawled at just as I do; I'm going to see him now before we go any further;" and I rose to leave.

"You look here; it would be just grand if my little woman was having a baby which, thank God, she is not, but for my sailors and Mountbatten's *Kelly* and the Fifth Destroyer Flotilla, to say nothing of Cahill's Coastal Command at Sullom Voe, what the hell does your 'Health' think they're playing at?"

I could not but agree that the situation was a little equivocal.

Good in his speciality the *locum tenent* surgeon undoubtedly was, but that was purely gynaecology and midwifery!

At the risk of wrecking the climax of this account I must, in all fairness, record that the self-same obstetrician, Archie Duncan, was later to earn a courageous D.S.C. in the very service which at the moment was renouncing him. He was later to be Professor of Obstetrics in the University of Wales.

* * * * *

When first I took over at the Gilbert Bain Hospital there was one aspect of the economy that caused me considerable worry, I learned that the Matron, who had been there for many years and was held in very high esteem, had lately transferred to a hospital in Aberdeenshire. Her place had been filled by another lady who had arrived but one week in advance of myself.

On surveying the hospital she had promptly tendered her resignation. Naturally, I was taken aback because, a newcomer myself, I still had to familiarise myself with the Shetland scene and its people. The Matron in such a cottage type of hospital is a vital pivot; there is no resident Houseman; she has not any retinue of assistants. All the supervision of nursing and care of the nurses' welfare, the control of maids, the linen management (and with no locally based laundry obviously this was to be a major problem) and a host of other responsibilities must come within the Matron's province. These duties too, have to be carried out in a small community where everyone knows everyone else and the hospital is a very conspicuous feature of public life; it follows that the Matron must possess exceptionally high qualities.

There must basically be understanding, tact, worldly knowledge and good technical skill. Nor can anyone doubt there must be mutual respect and co-operation between Surgeon and Matron. No petty bickerings or personal squabbles can be allowed to obtrude here.

My resolve now was that I must try and change the lady's attitude. Five days after my arrival Sunday dawned, a sparkling, delightful morning, one of those days when you wake up feeling good with a will to be up and doing. I paid an early visit and suggested to the restless Matron that perhaps she had had too long a spell on duty indoors; my sly suggestion was that we might have a motor run to Sumburgh Head, in the islands' southernmost part. This was agreed; the afternoon saw us off in a Ford V8, hired from Gansons' firm. Down the fine road we sped, skirting the high ground overlooking the sea inlets, the voes and wicks. We passed the off-shore Mousa, small but replete with historic interest. I pointed out the old tower or "Broch," as these so-called Pictish relics are named locally. I quoted the guide book which I had, with much forethought, quickly studied before this sortie! I declared with authority that this Broch was the most perfect example known; its walls I knew to be twelve feet thick and were built with an inward set thus giving the truncated appearance to the edifice. Hoping to inspire my companion with a new interest I recited from the Sagas of Northern Europe how Bjorn Bognjulfson, in Norway, had laid siege to the hand of Thora, Roald's daughter, but parental consent not forthcoming they eloped and took a ship for Iceland. Wrecked on the Isle of Mousa — the heather island, in Norse — they sheltered for the winter in the castle and eventually set sail for Iceland.

I expounded a lot more in which I made free with names such as the Earl of Atholl, Erland, Harald, Earl of Orkney, and for a modern touch told of the German Submarine Commander who, in the war of 1914-18, sheltered in the lee of Mousa in bad weather. With hatches open he put his ship's nose up on the shore. The crew stretched their legs and the larder was augmented by an odd sheep or two.

On went our car run; I lost no opportunity of declaiming on the scenic beauties; Fair Isle in the distance, then on the right the straggling ruins of Jarlshof, a village, I contend, of the Bronze Age. Recent excavations had unearthed weights of a peculiar ovoid shape, similar to those found by myself in the Mount Vernon "Cists" (coffins). When on the staff of the Anatomical Department of Glasgow

University I had been called upon to examine these and re-assemble the two thousand year old bones. The productions were housed in the west wing of Glasgow's Art Gallery, under the custodianship of my friend, the late Dr Tom Honeyman.

Our motor tour's apotheosis was a genial welcome by Mr and Mrs Leslie at the Sumburgh Hotel where an immense tea of home-baked comestibles was enjoyed.

On the return journey I made tentative attempts at reformation! I touched on the challenge of the appointment for any Matron; no one who would try to understand Shetland and its people would expect to find all the ancillary services of the Mayo Clinic just planted down in Lerwick. To my mind the acid test was that good results already came out of the existing hospital while newcomers like us might perhaps, with a fresh outlook, be able to exploit things a little more and suggest other lines of development; none of this could be done overnight.

I thought I detected signs of wavering, but, no, I had failed; all my carefully planned presentation of Shetland's potentialities had been in vain! Matron, a few days later, betook herself off.

The fates were kind. To my delight Mrs Frank Garriock, formerly Nurse Jamieson, nobly stepped into the breach. Wedded to a soldier husband she very naturally planned to join him in the South but, for my first four weeks, I was piloted through the intricacies of Shetland's interests; Mrs Garriock knew everyone in the islands and I found it solacing to work in such good company. When she rejoined her husband I reflected that Lieut. Garriock acquired a great asset but it was a sad loss for Gilbert Bain!

But *che serà serà!* Again the fates showed beneficence! Sister Thomasina Ann Pole, of Levenwick, was, fortunately for us, resident in Levenwick at this time. Mr Williamson (Bill Bill), the Hospital Trustees Honorary Secretary and I called on her at her home to discuss the situation. Miss Pole accepted our invitation and, with her installed in Matron's uniform, we looked forward confidently to smooth and efficient running of the hospital. This confidence in the Gilbert Bain's war-time Matron proved to be justified a thousandfold.

* * * * *

My first hospital charge was a six-foot blond giant obviously to me, of typically Scandinavian birth.

He was in fact a member of the crew of a Swedish vessel which had some days previously been torpedoed off the Faroe Islands, the Danish protectorate half-way to Iceland from Shetland.

He had been badly scalded by live steam and after succour by Dr Dahl, in Torshavn's hospital, had been shipped by fishing boat to Sullom Voe where 100 Wing, R.A.F. were at that time quartered on a hell-ship, *S.S. Manela*, commanded by Captain Cleaver, of the

British India Line, but long since put out to grass or to whatever watery pasture veteran ships retire!

The ship's surgeon had passed this almost inarticulate burned sufferer down to me on account of abscesses around his swollen face and neck.

Eager for my first blood, so to speak, I questioned him gently but closely on all the circumstances of the torpedoing of a neutral ship and of his sojourn in fascinating *Føroyar*.

Try as I would, however, in such smatterings as I then had of Swedish, Norwegian or even Russian, I could not make out my oedematous Viking's tongue.

On his return from an easement-giving visit to the operating theatre he appeared most anxious to convey something to me but could not write it down owing to the state of his hands.

I renewed my linguistic attack through the medium of the Swedish Vice-Consul, Lieutenant-Colonel Magnus Shearer, O.B.E., T.D., wearer of the blue riband of Swedish Knighthood from monarch Gustavus.

With all his ever-readiness to carry out an obligement the Shetland officer conducted a quite cursory interrogation, then told me with unaffected simplicity and a kindly restraint in his laughter; "He says that he cannot understand you at all but he's a British Consul passenger and wants to get back to Pontypool where ne belongs."

You see what I mean about the unwisdom of jumping to conclusions from preconceived ideas in Shetland?

*   *   *   *   *

With almost nightly torpedoings we soon became packed to overflowing with survivors and these of a great diversity of races; there could be Norwegian, Finnish, Swedish, Danish, Icelandic, Greek, Arab and British nationals all lying in juxtaposition in the one ward.

Many of these were in the category of near-irreversible shock and that one, in particular, recovered is more a tribute to his own Danish vitality, augmented by the skilled nursing he received, than to any resuscitative measures employed by me.

This chief engineer's vessel was torpedoed in the Atlantic on a wild January night of 1940. He was first blown out of his engine-room with the opening explosion and then hurled back in-board by the detonation of the succeeding tin fish. Then part of the cargo fell on top of him.

By this time his fragmented limbs scarcely permitted movement but he managed to slide into the icy, mountainous sea where, supported by his life-saving jacket, he was immersed for two hours before being picked up.

After a near-murderous but inescapable voyage in a small

storm-tossed fishing vessel he was landed, of necessity without the aid of any form of stretcher, at a westerly port of Shetland.

Even then his accumulating trauma was not concluded; he was questioned by the second-line intelligence authorities and would have fared worse but for the action of my good Man Friday, Geordie Fordyce, who put an abrupt stop to the ordeal by simply driving the archaic ambulance wagon, then in use, away and leaving its doors flapping open and the officious unintelligent young officer standing, anything but speechless!

A Norwegian seaman, escaping from Norway after we pulled out from Narvik, was five days in the sea following the sinking under him of his *shøyte*.* On being rescued he insisted on accompanying a unit of the Royal Navy to direct this craft to where he had last seen his skipper clinging to a piece of wreckage.

During this almost suicidal self-imposed undertaking he was shot through the abdomen from a marauding Heinkel.

The skipper was found, by all that was wonderful, and the Norwegian sailor required the repair of six bowel lacerations when his badly infected abdomen was subsequently explored. He now wears the Royal Norwegian Order of Saint Olav.

But not only was it the Scandinavians that took a lot of killing!

A pilot of the R.A.F., engaged in neutralising an enemy fighter aerodrome in southern Norway, during the Vaagso combined operation, had his lower limbs shattered by "flak" entering the bottom of his aircraft.

In the course of his subsequent evasive action, which he was just and no more able to take, he struck a rock and the starboard air-screw of his Blenheim went out of action.

He kept air-borne on one engine for some hundred miles and then came down in the sea; he was picked up more dead than alive by the Air-Sea Rescue Section.

Unhappily he had to lose a limb but, through it all, he was to gain in hospital something even more precious to him, and that by operations other than war-like!

He married the W.A.A.F. compatriot whom a kindly South Africa House sent up, at my request, to help him in the troubled course of his convalescence.

This pilot was a lecturer in Cape Town University and was, if not the first, as I think he was, at least amongst the earliest recipients of South Africa's D.F.C.s.

But not all casualties in my lengthy lists eventuated from war operations, at least not directly.

Here is an extract from a communication received from the commanding officer of a cruiser in Sullom Voe.

*Small motor fishing vessel.

It refers to the burial, with full military honours of a Surgeon Commander.

". . . . if conditions permitted I would come and thank you personally . . . . the sympathetic honours paid to the remains of our late shipmate. It is a great comfort and satisfaction to us of H.M.S. —— that in his departure he had paid to him the respect of the Navy and the Air Force and the old warriors of the British Legion . . . . please thank all those in Lerwick who took the places of those messmates and shipmates who were prevented by duty from attending.

"To you and your staff from our hearts — thank you."

Behind that lay a story of artificial-respiration administration, at first by relays of sick-berth attendants and latterly in the hospital iron-lung, over a period of twenty four hours.

But it was not to be; the eighteen grains of morphia, missing from the ship's poison-cupboard, proved too much for this fine up-standing senior officer as had the recurring bombardments and mutilation of comrades.

All hearts, though, were not solely concerned with destructive things as his commanding officer, in a Service which is not at all times severely silent, revealed in his letter no less than did the wreaths placed on the grave by the ladies of Lerwick.

Full military honours had, by order, to be paid to any personnel belonging to the enemy's armed forces who required burial from our hospitals. For this purpose we were supplied with a gargantuan swastika-defaced ensign, for draping over the coffin as it left the mortuary.

A Luftwaffe pilot, dead on arrival, was on his way out the gates, under this garish multi-coloured bunting.

A posse of aircraftsmen came to the "present" in the roadway on the word of command from their officer.

As the tumbril wheeled into Scalloway Road the local "village idiot" and a familiar figure craving pennies in the street, chose just at that moment to appear in all his raggedness.

Taking up his position at the head of the cortège he goose-stepped on in front, his right hand at the Nazi salute, and would have continued so to the cemetery had he not been stopped.

I am all in favour of respect to the dead and the honouring of the fallen foe but this posturing was really the most apt commentary, it seemed to me at the time, on the whole procedure!

CHAPTER XII

Since war's end I have met many German officers and, by all reasoning, they must have been gallant men serving their own code. One, in particular, now commands a hospital ship, patrolling the North Sea in the wake of his country's fishing fleet and I have many times operated on cases salvaged by him from his charges. In fact I have received through him official thanks from the Western Federal Government.

In war-time this officer commanded a German sea-raider until his capture and internment in Canada but in his heyday he was on close terms with the commander of the U-boat which penetrated Scapa Flow and sank *Royal Oak*.

I fully believe him that this commander was a fearless and clean fighter and have we not the testimony of Sir Winston Churchill to that same effect?

None the less, it was to be my experience in Shetland, as it was in World War One, that my personal contacts were with dirty, crafty, swashbuckling fighters.

Three of the crew of a Heinkel stand out as examples.

The remnants of that machine are still in Fair Isle where it was shot down to a pancake landing by a Hurricane from Sumburgh Head.

Some time before this downfall a German machine, in pursuance of the policy of neutralising all lighthouse-aid to shipping, had soared over the South Light. Its engine roar had caused little Margaret, aged fourteen, to run out and, in her innocence, to wave upwards in the friendliness of childhood.

She was shot to pieces.

Her mother, running out in her distraction, was to meet a similar end.

The little girl had, some time before that, been brought to me by lifeboat and had had a gangrenous appendix removed; we had all been much gratified that she had made a good recovery and could go home to Fair Isle for convalescence.

Whether or no the shot down machine was the one responsible for the killings must remain a matter of debate. As it was, a sturdy young Westphalian, the "tail-gun Charlie," was among those brought to me. He was sea-sick and terrified. Again, the lifeboat had functioned in a ninety-mile-an-hour gale to fetch the Germans to hospital.

At that time the R.A.F. Intelligence Officer was a man named Bishop. What his true rank was I never discovered because he was a protean sort of gentleman, who, chameleon-like, changed his rank according to that of the prisoner, whom he happened to be interrogating.

For myself, I had, many years earlier, been trained in a Field Reconnaissance Unit and I remembered enough of the gentle (sic) art of questioning the captives we were often sent out to take. I was only too willing to assist friend Bishop in all his inquiries.

Added to this, it must be obvious that any surgeon, in an operating threatre, just about to wield the knife, provides a powerful incentive to the most fanatical young Nazi to tell the truth!

Consequently I have my own views. Be they right or wrong it was incontestible that the same race was involved and I was now faced with the duty of restoring to health members of that race which was responsible for murdering my little patient. I carried out my obligations as a healer but I was conscious of great emotional turmoil within myself; my early training as a killer was with difficulty submerged.

Perhaps, in deference to the Geneva Convention, I should enlarge no further on this score!

Suffice it to say that this young *Unteroffizier* recovered from his operation but not before he had complained that the hospital bed assigned to him was too hard!

Fair Isle people may rest assured that he was adequately made recumbent in the way he merited and I had Bishop's assurance that he did, in fact, make a very considerable contribution of value to our war effort!

His pilot had on Fair Isle attempted to fire the machine by discharging his revolver into the fuel tanks. He was prevented in this by the men of Fair Isle. He was housed temporarily in the cooler in Lerwick. There he complained of a sore back, and he was brought down to me for examination. After X - ray and other examination I decided that there was mighty little wrong with this arrogant and haughty representative of the *Herrenvolk,* at least in a physical sense.

At that time we had been reading a lot about the splendid clothing and equipment which Germany supplied to her flying men.

My patient, however, as he stood sulkily in my office in the Gilbert Bain Hospital, presented to me a sorry sort of spectacle clad as he was in a pair of a rough kind of moleskin trousers and coarse khaki shirt.

Just as contemptuous as he, I flipped his cheap, narrow braces with my finger and said; "If that's all the Luftwaffe can provide I don't think much of it!"

The reply came from Chief Constable Tom Stuart, who was standing by. He drew himself up to his full six feet two and interposed with great dignity; "Sir, that is the clothing our Home Office provides for prisoners on remand."

It appeared that old Bishop was away with all the Hun-owned stuff to be searched for sewn-in maps and the like.

Anyway it was I who had to bear the brunt of all the subsequent correspondence in reference to Baron von Richthofen's complaints that I had pinched ten Reichsmarks, a wristlet watch and a swastika emblem!

* * * * *

There were, in the course of the whole war, several persons suspected of being engaged in subversive activity on behalf of the enemy; with some I came into contact. In the case of three of them I was glad to be asked to assist in their apprehension.

A very personable young lady arriving in the van of the four thousand escapees from Norway, whom we passed through, came under suspicion for a time and it fell to my not unwilling efforts to prove her to be a genuine patriot.

Two were out-and-out spies.

One, in the dress of a humble A.C. One, was, after his landing by rubber dinghy, speedily winkled out from the masses of similarly clad airmen by the innermost security ring exercising such ingenuity that they earned my complete respect and admiration.

Again deference must be paid to a certain convention of 1906 but it can be safely remarked that the enemy was the first to honour their agreement in the breach as well as in the observance!

The second, in this category, was a member of the German *Sicherheitspolizei*, in a marine section, of which the nearest equivalent translation I can think of is River Police.

The security service to which he belonged, *Sicherheitsdienst*, was originally merely the intelligence arm of the S.S. but later earned unforgettable dishonour for their distinguishing initials, S.D.

In Admiral Raeder's own words they were indoctrinated with the theory of the master race, the *Fuhrer* principle, "the whole destiny of German Youth — to die for Hitler; the great tradition of death for a holy cause, knowing that with their blood they will lead the way towards the freedom of their dreams."

The form, in our area, was to plant these idealistic gentry on neutral shipping which was in all probability doomed to be torpedoed within the environs of Scapa Flow. The hope was that the agent, preferably wounded, would be, as a survivor, admitted to a hospital.

Where better for a bogus neutral to pick up bits of sea-lore

F

and defence arrangements than among the sympathetic brotherhood in such a place?

My particular quarry bit the dust by letting his Teutonic "Old Adam" reveal his true Prussian lechery; he interpreted his "holy cause" as being to make a pass at my nurses, licking his Aryan chops the while!

His blood-spilling death towards the freedom of his dreams was unattended by any audience attuned to value his last "Heil Hitler!"

Another man, a great listener to Lord Haw-Haw, was a "protester." He was, of all things, a chief petty officer though but a Fleet Reservist.

He blew the gaff during a display of his violent temper; in my presence he denounced the First Lord and stoutly defended Hitler's would-be girl friend, Unity Mitford, member of the gallant but unfortunate Lord Redesdale's family.

He claimed to belong to some esoteric society. His outburst in the Grand Hotel, where I lived, led to his removal for disciplinary inquiry.

The same little Unity was a neurote. She was a self-appointed "Adolf-acolyte" and managed to make her charming way to his side. ("You should see the blue of his eyes.")

Eva Braun, however, found Unity *unecht* and consequently, with the panther-like spring of the female, had U-born interloper plugged with a very noisy Luger right on her well-coiffed little pate.

For La Mitford this was quite too *uneben* and she came home through Switzerland, on a stretcher.

Even then she was not to finish her consorting with considerably bad *hombres;* her little ruse, of which we were duly apprised by the appropriate quarter, was to masquerade in Red Cross uniform.

Her ultimate fate was to die of a meningeal complication in the West Highland Cottage Hospital, Oban, where I chanced to be at the time.

                    *   *   *   *   *

With the rape of Norway Shetland was a willing haven for loyal Norwegians in transit. Originally my good friends, Oslo-born Mrs Hanka Adie and her husband received these people out of the goodness of their hearts. Later things were put on a more official basis under the aegis of the Home Office and the Adies' beneficent work was given adequate recognition, largely through the intervention of Trygve Lie, outstanding Norwegian politician who escaped to England in 1940 where he joined H.M. King Haakon and occupied high executive position in the exiled Government. He was, of course, in 1946 to become Secretary-General to the Uinted Nations.

With these Norwegians thronging into Shetland there was, of

course, considerable alertness to intercept any undesirable elements that might be of their number.

Into this atmosphere of wariness and amongst the very first arrivals came Toni Dahl, a professed medical student from the State Hospital in Oslo.

Toni is a Norwegian beauty, of the high cheek-boned, fair-haired supple type. She arrived over in a whaler in company with a man in the uniform of a Royal Norwegian Naval Surgeon-Lieutenant, who did not make a very good impression. He borrowed some shirts from me and from that day to this has never been seen or heard of by me!

Toni herself was clad in the greatcoat of a German *Stahlhelmer* and claimed to have crossed the Telemark Mountains of southern Norway on skis, travelling by moonlight and hiding up by day, a total of three weeks being taken for the journey. "He has no further use for it," was her smiling explanation of how she came by the blue-grey overcoat.

After her stormy crossing to Shetland she was naturally pretty well all in but once she was tended for this her perfectly clear sun-tanned complexion and good state of nutrition raised doubts in some quarters as to credibility of her whole account.

Added to that and quite unconsciously, as it happened, she put both her dainty feet right in it by saying she would like to come and work in a local hospital!

As can be appreciated after the considerable brouhaha in the matter of *Sicherheitspolizei,* Security in Shetland was not a little allergic to foreign nationals who coveted entry into sick houses!

It was at this point that I was asked if I would examine her background.

As a preliminary I invited her to come up and see me with a view to having her blood tested for purposes of blood donation.

This she readily did and in the course of our chatting I probed her knowledge of anatomy, with which science, according to her claims, she should have been familiar.

Naming a structure, the Brachial Plexus, which is an intricate assortment of branching nerves, for all the world like Clapham railway junction, I laughingly asked her if she remembered enough to draw it.

Without a word she took paper and pencil and drew out the whole pattern with an exactitude for which I myself should have needed a text-book in confirmation.

Then, "for good measure," as she added; "here's the Cervical Plexus too."

There was no shadow of doubt! Toni was a *pukka* medical student.

There were other points; she knew all about my friends, Doctor Johan Heimbeck and Professor Hölst of Oslo.

Toni was in the clear and off she went to Craiglockhart Hospital, Edinburgh, where the British Government gave Professor Hölst beds to practise his thoracic surgery.

He became supreme medical head of all the Free Norwegian Forces and Toni married the V.D. expert, a Norwegian Surgeon-Commander.

*   *   *   *   *

Years later, in July, 1945, immediately after the Liberation, I was a guest in Oslo at the celebrations attending King Haakon's birthday and on that evening I was of Toni's personal party, along with her newly returned husband, at the Liberation Ball, held in Oslo's luxury Hotel Bristol. I had been accommodated in this same lush hostelry, in a suite of which the bedroom contained two beds, a gesture of hospitality that could not be rivalled, I always thought! But for the brilliant function downstairs, the celebrated mirrored hall was at the exclusive disposal of the Norwegian patriots. No allied officer could attend in uniform and would only be admitted, in any case, if he were the guest of a Norwegian. This elegent apartment had been the stamping ground for Terboven, the Gauleiter, with his merry men and in consequence had been boycotted by Osloan society.

Tonight was to mark the return for the first time of the latter and an orchestra was provided by the National State Opera. The company was largely composed of Norway's own surviving national heroes and heroines of the Resistance.

In this scene, then, I was to commit the greatest gaffe of all time.

It had been seen fit by the Norwegian authorities to provide me with a liaison officer, a young naval lieutenant. This was a wise precaution as far as I was concerned for the city was teeming with rather trigger-happy young members of the Home Front who were now in open possession of firearms and explosives largely supplied to them by the war-time "Shetland Bus."

Indeed at the actual Capitulation the Norwegians insisted that the military governor, General von Falkenhorst, wearing full decorations and attended by his aides, surrender to an armed stripling of seventeen, dressed in plus fours, outside the medieval fortress of Akerhus, symbol of Oslo's independence and burial ground of many executed patriots.

A photograph, banned in this country, had been taken of this and, at the time of my arrival, the shop windows contained little else but it. (I am looking at a copy this moment!)

The consequence was that every youngster saw himself in

the guise of this Liberator and bands of them roamed about ready to loose off at anyone who did not answer their challenge in their own *Landsmaal* speech.

There was no end of quislings not yet rounded up; in fact during my residence the blond young *fruken* at a desk in the hotel, to whom I was instructed to apply for a Mercedes-Benz from the transport pool, whenever I wanted it, was collected and imprisoned. Quisling himself could be seen daily at exercise in the City Gaol.

Municipal police were not yet re-organised, law and order being in the hands of scattered patrols of the First Airborne Division and a few jeep-fuls of American "snow-drops."

On hearing that I was to attend the Hotel Bristol Ball my young liaison man, in a flush of enthusiasm, eagerly inquired if he might fetch along his fiancée whom he had not seen until now, after three years' separation.

Quite unthinkingly and very foolishly I answered: "By all means."

Now, I feel sure that any lady readers I may have will be quick to realise the enormity of my offence.

This was to have been Toni's night; here she was a sort of Mrs Gerald Legge of Oslo, and quite a national figure, entertaining a brand new patriot husband along with a representative from that Little Norway, the Shetland Isles, in the company of the élite of her native soil.

Furthermore, like all her other active feminine associates she possessed no evening raiment "fit to wear."

With the other Amazonion patriots there had been a little ploy to wear hats instead. These had been meticulously conveyed by returning warriors from all over the world on insistent orders, and in many cases, neither the fitting nor the ensemble effect was at all appropriate.

Toni herself wore an absurdity from Paris, a little black affair with a bewitching eye-veil.

Now, into her special little party, as she bowed and shook hands, keeping a watchful eye open for Crown Prince Olav all the time, I brought, or was responsible for bringing a complete stranger to her, an animated teenager all dressed up in chiffon and tulle!

Toni was wild, I saw quite well, and never would I have believed how devastatingly withering can a lacy eye-veil look when tossed at a blundering male over a perfect little *retroussé* nose!

She declined to speak to me until I managed to exploit my popularity with the manager of the hotel. This *empressement* arose from the fact that I had, on arrival, presented him with a large round tin of New Zealand butter, acquired on the destroyer which had borne me from Rosyth to Stavanger and although now a trifle rancid in the July heat of Oslo, was none the less manna from heaven for the fat-starved Norwegian.

After a little coloquy with him it was assured that Toni's champagne glass was never empty — there were lashings of that benison, re-filched from the extensive Hun-cellars, although the food was limited to crayfish, eels and one piece of toast!

The therapeutic measure proved effective and my beautiful hostess thawed.

Still later, I gave a post-party in my suite to a group of nicely-chosen patriots who were making every endeavour to make up for lost time on the multitude of bottles largely of Polish origin, I noted, which the Senior Naval Officer, Hans Nordhuus, had evoked in response to my modest request for a few drinks for the lads and lassies.

I deemed the moment appropriate to pump Toni as to how in fact the German Stahlhelmer, whose blue-grey coat she had come by, really met his end.

Again she closed up like a clam and I was back where I started!

*   *   *   *   *

There was something like four thousand escapees, of whom I have any knowledge, who came through Shetland.

An outstanding visitor was the poet Nordahl Grieg, grandson of composer Edouard. A striking figure with aesthetic features and long dark hair he was later to lose his life, shot down in a bomber over Berlin, when he sought to obtain local colour for his work.

I saw him in a dimly lit Nisson hut near Scalloway. Most of his audience were of the Independent Naval Force, and included Leif Larsen. The taut, tense faces of these patriots shone beneath the paltry beam of a hurricane lamp. The poet inspired with his own verse; "when the air of Norway is clean again," he cried passionately in his peroration.

Tragedy attended many of the attempted crossings in fragile craft. On the other hand even a tiny baby, in her Grannie's arms, passed through my hands after a hazardous crossing in a small boat.

A vivid picture of Norwegian defiance was established by the Bergen ferry boat as she was berthed alongside at Victoria Pier; most of her superstructure was gone but aft, the Norwegian Marine pennant fluttered bravely. Below the spar wearing it there stood erect, in the stern, a shining white retort to the Nazis, it seemed to be, in all its nakedness!

This was an appliance of domestic use frequently associated with the well-known Barrhead firm — Messrs Shanks!

CHAPTER XIII

Quartered in the Grand Hotel I enjoyed especially one particular interlude; this was the periodic and unheralded entry of the 100-Wing pilots from Sullom Voe into our midst. Wise Wing Commander Cahill (later to be Group Captain, D.F.C., A.F.C.), appreciated full well the desirability of allowing his juniors regular liberty boats to bring them in from their grimy home, S.S. *Manela*, anchored in the voe. Even one night's respite was beneficial and as for the wives, resident like me in the hotel, the joy of re-union was manifest. I admired these young men, with their "prang" and "wizard" vocabulary; all were fresh faced, athletic and keen. I noted too that had the Grand Hotel been dependent on them for revenue from the sale of intoxicating liquors, right soon would the proprietor have been facing bankruptcy!

One piquant incident remains in my recollection. A coal-carrying vessel, *Sea Venture*, had been sunk by gunfire from a submarine off the Outstack, the most northerly land of the U.K. The Lerwick lifeboat had been summoned by a London flying boat, the type of aircraft — outmoded and slow — which originally comprised 100 Wing, Coastal Command. For two days in a gale, the Lerwick boat searched and eventually, attracted by a chance light, had found all hands, safe but chilled to the bone by the cold and wet, on the island of Muckle Flugga. In their searching in the dark, the lifeboatmen met destroyers who, very naturally, were most inquisitive with embarrassing searchlights. In these days everyone afloat treated all strangers with profound suspicion until credentials were proved. I myself, making passage to the island of Uyea on an M.L. of the Royal Navy, witnessed a near disaster for a British submarine, sheltering cosily in a voe of the mainland; she was too dilatory, when challenged, in returning the recognition signal of the day. The Captain of my ship was all set to sink him when a belated message flashed over that they "were only having their breakfast in peace!" Ruse after ruse was adopted by the German submarine commanders to emulate the decoying tactics of our formerly famous Q-Ships. Even the Union Jack was painted on their decks at times.

The crew of *Sea Venture* were re-clothed and housed in

Lerwick. A party of eight of their number were honoured guests at the centre table in the dining room of the Grand Hotel. They yarned and chatted away what time they consumed our sorely needed wartime fare. "Haddock, sausages and egg." A single-ringed youthful Flying Officer entered and took a seat. His routine order voiced, he grinned over and enquired: "Get in all right, Chaps?" "Aye fine," said the engineer at our table; "but we couldn't understand yon Morse thing o' yours."

"Never mind," came the nonchalant reply; "I've got some wizard photos of your ship in flames!"

"Oh, have ye now? That's good."

In a pregnant silence the attack on the haddock, sausage and egg was resumed.

The gaps in what this little snippet of badinage concealed can be filled in. A lurching collier, bound for Trondjeim, suddenly attacked by shellfire in a howling gale; one boat smashed to pieces by a direct hit, shells screaming over, one after another; seamen escaping the Scylla of cordite to challenge the Charybidis of brine. The ship in flames left behind as the hands are hard put to it to keep their boats afloat. Suddenly there comes a flying boat seeking vengeance on the U-boat (now dived to safety). All the pilot can do is to signal encouragement to the mariners and summon aid from elsewhere. What these men had to say in the matter of this saga of the sea was but the chaffing interchange in the dining room.

*   *   *   *   *

"Grimy" well describes the condition of poor old *Manela,* erstwhile B.I. cruise ship. She had to stow in her holds all the bombs and other ammunition; also her own bunkers and victualling. A trying ordeal it was for both officers and other ranks. It was particularly taxing for the latter — the officers and sergeant-pilots were putting in strenuous hours of flying and were only too glad to rest when occasion offered. For the non-flying personnel there were their duties of ferrying, refuelling, rigging and all the other innumerable tasks, but there were long periods of idleness when these men, unaccustomed to life on board ship, and a dirty one at that, had nothing to do but sit, smoke, read and talk. Wing Commander Cahill was handicapped to some extent by actions of mine, in his efforts to combat ennui in his command. Firstly, I removed his physical training instructor for operation on the maxillary antrum. Then I brought his marine Warrant officer to hospital on account of mastoid disease. Soon the 7th Gordon Highlanders departed for their training area and this deprived the Royal Air Force of their opponents on the football field!

The mere business of coming ashore was distasteful to many of these land-reared men. The pinnace would be brought alongside but then from the rickety companion ladder nice judgment was required to ensure safe alighting on board the little boat. Then, depending on the tide, and with footwear removed, they would have to wade 100 yards to reach a desolate shore. Service men have told me that 100 Wing had the worst war station in the Air Force — worse even than Orkney! On my periodic visits to the ship I noticed one further discouragement to diversion — this a relic of palmier days; "Passengers are warned not to play cards with strangers."

There was a ship's surgeon whose duties concerned the ship's company as distinct from the Air Force personnel. Poor old doctor! He was nearer eighty than seventy and had been anxious to do his bit. He had been told by the pundits in the South that there was a 10,000 ton ship cruising in Scottish waters; how would he like to join her?

Cruising, ye Gods!

In my talks with Flight Lieutenant Carson, the Medical Officer, I made the point that these men would have been better off mentally had they been lying off Heligoland Bight, right in the jaws of the tiger but, as it was, they were so near and yet so far from Lerwick, which, to them, represented a metropolis with all its temporal joys including contact with the fair sex. So near and yet so far can be a most tantalising predicament.

Another factor had an influence. These men were sitting on a veritable volcano of ammunition and, for many weeks, had no protection in the shape of anti-aircraft ordnance. Periodic reconnaissance was made by hostile aircraft and no doubt detailed photographs were taken. Daily there was expected a downpour of high explosives which would blow them, and Sullom Voe too, all to Kingdom come!

For some reason the enemy did not attack (except for an abortive bombing on one New Year's morn) and many thought the Germans were content to leave the old London flying boats unmolested. From the Teutonic point of view they were much preferable to the Spitfires, Skuas, Sunderlands and Catalinas, which in the fulness of time, arrived to supplant the old "crates." In the matter of protection, too, after the initial defencelessness, very new and "hush-hush" anti-aircraft cruisers arrived; H.M.S. Sheffiield and Newcastle.

Until these more confident days eventuated I saw many sick from the S.S. Menela. These would come into hospital, ill men, worn down by the suspense and conditions of life. Some reacted by surliness, some by lethargy; others by malingering and even by obstructionism. All were handled, apart from any surgical condition they might have, by psychological understanding. Tingwall Hospital proved invaluable for this type of war exhaustion; the tranquility was salutary — Cahill told me that when such of these men were deemed fit to return to duty their work was carried out in a manner beyond reproach.

In parenthesis it can be recorded that Tingwall Hospital's peaceful atmosphere helped recovery in quite a different order of patient but also one suffering from continual stress — the undercover agent from occupied Norway. Of these people we kept no records.

Some there were from *Manela* who were transferred by me to hospitals in the South, labelled unfit for further service with 100 Wing. These were men for whom I had nothing but sympathy. Men of fighter squadrons and members of combatant land forces might scoff at this but it was my belief that my misfits would have fought well had they been called upon so to do in different environment.

Friendly and all as I became with the Senior Naval Officer, Captain Inglis, I could never see eye to eye with him in this matter. His view was that they were pampered. "Let them have a spell in a destroyer on North Sea patrol and they'll soon see what discomfort really is," he was given to saying.

My contention was that they would have come through that undoubted ordeal with credit. They were just not strong enough for inactivity.

One patient who intrigued me greatly was a Chief Petty Officer based on the armed trawler "Sea Breeze." He was a diver who had been on duty around *Manela*. This man was a powerful, swarthy, good looking fellow and, along with one other, he held the record for depth in the regulation suit. His complaint was lumbago, but my private opinion was that he was just fed up and needed a rest. I prescribed the infra-red lamp and massage; the efficacy of his treatment was abundantly revealed when I met him on the evening of his discharge from hospital. He was marching along Commercial Street, all the bewildering golden sleeve-regalia further enhanced by an extremely pretty girl on either arm!

Even record divers had their moments of elevation it seemed!

CHAPTER XIV

Narvik!

With Shetland but some one hundred and eighty miles from the nearest point on the Norwegian coastline we saw a great assortment of maritime casualties during the major occupation of that country, limping vessels that just managed to make the sanctuary of our harbours.

The destroyer *Eclipse*, with forty feet of her after-end blown away and an equal number of dead on board, presented a bizarre appearance with her guns twisted into grotesque corkscrews pointing skywards.

For the disposal of her dead we had to ask for a mortuary ship to be sent up, the first of its kind I ever saw.

A touching memorial service was held in the Parish Church, St. Columba's.

Other destroyers could be seen out in the stream, visibly going down by the water-line, what time feverish activity in patching up holes could be witnessed as small repair ships busied themselves all around.

There was the destroyer sea-battle of Rombaks and Oftot Fjords wherein Warburton-Lee ("I attack at dawn") youthful-looking Captain of *H.M.S. Hardy,* whom 1 had seen but a few days previously, thrilled the nation by blowing to smithereens the numerically superior German force.

He was to lose his life on a raft which his crew launched to convey him from his stricken vessel, "like a little expeditionary force all on its own," as was said, to the small Norwegian village of Ballengen, on the Oftot Fjord.

The posthumous Victoria Cross awarded him is one of the proudest in the Navy's history.

This action was the prelude to the land and sea operation against the iron-ore port. That combined operation did succeed but only after painstaking weeks of preparation, in which composite forces, the Polish Highland Brigade, the French Chasseurs Alpins and Foreign Legion, along with the Norwegian Fifth Division, under General Ruge, all took part.

The gallant commander of the British land and sea arms, Admiral of the Fleet, the Earl of Cork and Orrery, G.C.B., G.C.V.O.,

his flag flying on *H.M.S. Aurora,* after a personal reconnaissance over
Narvik in a Swordfish aircraft, would have made the assault months
earlier, despite the four feet of snow but his Army commander,
Major-General Mackesy was deterred by the state of the terrain

Who knows but that the Old Man was right and that the
subsequent evacuation of the captured peninsular, enforced by the
dramatic events occurring in France and the Netherlands, need not
have taken place?

To this day, however, he declines to re-open the subject of
"what might have been."

The affectionate use of the term "Old Man" is justified for
it was he who, after Narvik, was detailed to Shetland, to assume
command of the defence of the islands and to organise them for
the invasion that was deemed to be imminent and for which, by
all Intelligence reports, the Wehrmacht was making hurried preparation in the way of accumulating ships and barges in such ports as
Bergen and Trondjeim, just opposite to us.

To these the Royal Air Force gave concentrated attention and
it may be thus vitiated a descent on Lord Cork's command.

That he was never called upon to defend the islands is a
fact to which he appends the qualifying adjective "unfortunate,"
a sentiment most decidedly not reflected in the feelings of us others
who were there!

When commanding in Norway the Admiral had decided on
land headquarters at Harstadt, on the island of Hinnoy in the Lofoten
group. In order to facilitate matters for his ally, General Ruge
requisitioned a suitable and commodious house in the town.

This chanced to belong to a medical man, prominent in the
Lofotens and, not unnaturally, he was most indignant at being displaced. In the end the matter was amicably settled but not before
Lord Cork had brought all his Hibernian charm to bear on the
disgruntled one for his Lordship possessed an abundance of that
grace in addition to a goodly supply of the martinet's stringencies
for the wrong-doer!

Now, in Shetland, there was to be repeated a similar impasse
with the profession, in this case me, although not in respect of my
dwelling place.

This came about because in conformity with my original
mandate from the Secretary of State to send an appreciation of
the whole picture in Shetland, I had been sending considerably more,
literally a bombardment of requests, in fact, that were anything
but appreciative of the hospital situation.

In the forefront of essentials was the demand for additional
accommodation for the sick, not only of the Services but of the
civilian population.

I was in a constant state of worry over the latter for not only did we expect heavy air-raid casualties but the accumulating martialdom of the islands was inevitably attended by an increasing accident rate, not only from road misadventures but from explosions of stored depth charges, torpedoes, anti-sweep devices and other contact mines swept up on the foreshores and all manner of further disasters, enemy-occasioned or otherwise.

The priceless target for acquisition, as I saw it, was a comely and commodious building which had been gifted by the beneficent donor whose name it bears, the Bruce Hostel. This is owned by the Education Authority and is used to house young ladies from the country districts who are in attendance at the adjacent Anderson Institute.

This, the secondary school, was originally gifted by a granduncle of my wife's, Arthur Anderson, founder of the Peninsular and Oriental Line of steamships. It was later to become a hundred-bedded Army hospital.

Much opposition, prior to Lord Cork's arrival, had, very understandably, been forthcoming to any interference with the fine Bruce Hostel, the apple, so to speak, of the Authority's eye, with all its beautiful interior woodwork.

Already, too, the educationists had been prevailed upon, (somewhat compulsorily, I fear!) to part with their Central School Gymnasium which was by now the Naval Auxiliary Sick-Quarters. This was in two pavilions, the larger occupied by the patients, the smaller was devoted to ancillary services, kitchens, ablution, etcetera.

The one end of this was retained by the school administrators as a classroom in which "the little ones could learn their woodwork."

Little did the kindly dominies think that with twenty naval ratings abed next door the little ones were to learn much of life that was considerably divorced from woodcraft!

In regard to the final plum, by dint of much lobbying, an amicable arrangement, without the enforcement of the power to requisition, had been reached and the coveted Hostel was ours.

The preliminary re-arrangements had been contrived and the massive battery of sterilising plant was already in position adjacent to the improvised operating theatre.

My mistake was in not having at least one patient already housed there when *Aurora* bearing Lord Cork steamed into Lerwick!

One look at my *pièce de resistance* he cast.

"This is my fighting-top," he announced and brooked no further parley.

Thereupon his fourteen members of a staff, with an equivalent number of telephones, took up station to repel all boarders.

As soon as I could penetrate the barbed wire of brass I bearded the lion in his den, the fine, harbour-viewing room, in fact, which I regarded as my own but now offensively labelled; "Admiral's Cabin."

"Far too exposed for a hospital; it's the outstanding landmark from seaward"; was the brush-off offered to me.

With considerable temerity but having heard of the cowed Lofoten medico I then suggested that such vulnerability made the Hostel quite inappropriate for the hierarchy dedicated to the defence of the islands.

"I'm used to it," put the closure on that avenue for the moment.

Then I requested permission to have the use of his scrambled telephone for a call to Edinburgh.

"What's that for?" he demanded.

"To complain about your action, sir—to St. Andrew's House," and I put the emphasis on the name of Scotland's administrative citadel.

His immaculate and naturally marcelled ginger hair was quite unruffled at the dire threat but there was an appreciative twinkle in the noble eye.

"Go ahead then;" and he turned to his Chief of Staff; "Nicholson; see that this saw-bones gets every facility to telephone his people."

With that he donned the peaked cap, with its multi-gilded cloth of gold, lifted a silver-topped, black malacca cane and spared a final word for me:

"Adjust your tie!"

Then he walked out.

From the high-ranking civil servant with whom I presently made contact in St. Andrew's House came this advice for Sisyphean toil; "Pay no attention to those people, Mr Lamont, the Navy's always inclined to bluff. You stand up for your rights."

"Will you come up here and do the standing then, for I'm whacked?" I replied.

In due course I ushered the Principal Secretary into that sinister cabin; he was about to "show them."

He was out in less than three minutes, the punctilious tail of red tape well and truly between the legs.

"It's no use, Mr Lamont; they've got A1 priority and you'll need to go elsewhere."

All the same, that night, Lord Cork asked me to dine with him off his crested plate.

In the final event we went to Tingwall, the site of Shetland's ancient parliament and there, around the Free Church manse, vested in the Trustees of the Church of Scotland and of which the incumbent was serving nobly as a paratrooper chaplain, was built hutted Tingwall Emergency Hospital which became famous in its unique situation as the United Kingdom's most northerly house of healing.

It stood at the head of a placid loch, often fished by Lord Cork and his staff.

Another small sick bay, located at the top of Gullet's Brae, the hill running up from the Gilbert Bain, was set up by the Norwegian forces. In charge was Surg. Lieut. Dramsdahl, a Russo-Finnish War veteran. Another Royal Norwegian Naval establishment was an Officers' Club in the premises now occupied by Shetland's Consulting Surgeon, Ordgarff House. Many distinguished escapees were temporarily accommodated there. Among them was Professor Hölst, from the Oslo University Chair of Surgery. He was thereafter made medical supremo of all Norwegian forces when he was given wards in Craiglockhart Hospital, Edinburgh.

In the Lerwick area the army was a long time getting into its stride in the matter of their own hospitals. The first one was a mere hutted arrangement out the North Road under the care of Lieut. Summers, R.A.M.C.

Eventually they occupied the Anderson Institute with a Lieut.-Col. Fox in command. I say "Lieut.-Col." but as often as not he was "Major." The reason was that the number of occupied beds was wont to fall periodically below one hundred, the Army's regulation number to warrant the higher rank.

Poor Fox reacted, understandably, by considerable disgruntlement each time these vicissitudes downgraded him. It followed, of course, that he evinced some resentment at the preference shown by the Air Force and Naval Medical Officers to utilise the civilian Emergency Medical Service. His manoeuvering, I was sorry to hear from General Manifold, Army Medical Services, when a guest at his Edinburgh home in Corstorphine, earned for him some unpopularity at Scottish Command.

Another medical establishment was set up at Sumburgh by the army. This was in a requisitioned house which was really equipped for very little other function than that of a reception centre. Despite this limitation one youthful R.A.M.C. subaltern flabbergasted me by asking me if I would lend him an electric cautery as he proposed to do some operating on piles!

On my query as to what manner of anaesthetic was to be employed he replied quite nonchalantly; "Oh, ether." "Then you must be prepared to blow the whole place up once you start," I told him and curtly declined his request.

At the same time I thought it was my duty to report this irresponsibility to the appropriate quarter. To my relief, within days, that enterprising young gentleman was dispatched overseas where, no doubt, he would find scope for lesser imaginative talents!

Through time, all these hospital dispositions came to cater

adequately for the needs of the Forces. It remained a feature, though, that officers, when sick, preferred Tingwall!

The civilian population were thus no longer in danger of being crowded out from their own hospital and it remains my proud boast that never once, during all the war, had a non-Service patient to be denied institutional care when required.

There came, however, on one tempestuous night an occasion when our resources were strained to the uttermost and a clamant demand for accommodation was met by the utilisation of both the Tingwall and the Isolation Hospitals.

This eventuated from the near-demolition of Lerwick's Gilbert Bain.

So fierce was the hurricane that a large ship's rusting boiler, said to have rested on the sea's bottom, in the Brei Wick, for fifteen years, was snatched from its tomb and hurled up on the foreshore some two hundred yards distant from our hospital.

But, at seven o'clock that night, the first of seven other things was dashed upon the self-same rocks; the safety zone from these death-scattering machines is reckoned by the Mine's Disposal Section to be eight houndred yards.

The recurrent detonations were ear-splitting; the green and violet luminosity accompanying them flared up to the whole cloud-filled firmament like some vast corposant, St. Elmo's Fire in the sundered rigging of the fearsome night.

The dwelling houses lining the road round the Wick were stoutly constructed to withstand the onslaughts of Shetland weather but this was more than they could endure; freakish vagaries of blast hurtled round corners to tear out windows and foundations at far distant points. Massive links from mine-mooring chains were found half a mile away in the town.

And in the dislustred dark which followed there went on the contrapuntal howl of the storm as it whipped the sea-wrack aloft with frenzied trails.

The solid little hospital, defiant in its good stone masonry, reinforced for air-raids by sand bags and timber baulks, suffered grievously. All glass and plaster work came tumbling down in a shower of débris.

The electrical circuits failed and right on top of the recumbent patients descended all the wall-fittings.

By the light of emergency hurricane lamps I toured the wards, thinking to assuage all panic. I need not have worried — there was none.

In the row of disrupted beds on the female side I saw one patient sitting up, the flex and wall-bracket of a brass fitting festooned round her neck and shoulders.

"We can take it," called Mrs Theo Kay, wife of a prominent local ornithologist, business man and yachtsman who himself had dared the peril to come up and help.

In the male ward my greatest problem in the evacuation came from three airmen and their pilot, survivors of an air-crash in the island of Yell.

These were multiple fracture cases and the orthopaedic arrangement of Balkan Beams and extension apparatus had come to great harm.

They co-operated fully and in spite of vast discomfort remained cheerful and encouraging to me throughout their ordeal.

To and fro, into the holocaust around the Wick itself went old Geordie Fordyce in his dilapidated veteran yellow ambulance, soon to have its windscreen and all other glass broken into fragments.

At one point he arrived with a great chunk of iron embedded in the rended tyre of his off-side wheel but, no matter, out he came from his seat to help the A.R.P. Rescue Squad, led by a school-teacher named Murray, to lift the stretchers and convey the patients to the comparative safety of the Isolation Hospital, up on the hill.

One woman, in actual labour, he lifted from her bed in the midst of the reverberations at their deadliest height. The child was born safely.

In the operating theatre, assisted by Sister Isa Carnegie, I had to find time to give immediate attention to slashed and bleeding scalps and faces.

One terrific blast brought down the ceiling and sent us both, along with the patient, helter skelter across the tiled floor.

Isa, who had been breaking open a tube of cat-gut, picked herself up, her burnished hair, alas, no longer an aureole of gold but rather now a dishevelment of tangled corn, stretched out her hand to me; "Your ligature, sir," was all she said as she shook and ejected the powdered plaster from her mouth.

Surgeon Lieutenant-Commander Percy Coats, along with Chief Constable Tom Stuart, were both volunteers who did yeoman service that night: Warden Tom Manson, Honorary Doctor of Laws and proprietor of the "Shetland News" was in the A.R.P. Control Centre where the lady to be my wife was an emergency telephonist; he made valiant efforts to direct the ambulance but the demands far exceeded the facilities available but none-the-less he was one of those there to help.

In all we were miraculously fortunate in having but the one fatality.

In the comparative peace that came with dawn's advent, I surveyed the empty scene from amidst the ruins of Pompeii.

The four walls of the pathetic but valiant little building still

G

stood and it was a matter of marvelling by me that feverish activity
on the part of local builders had the institution functioning once
more in a matter of weeks. The Shetlander certainly *does* know
how to get a spurt on when necessity arises!

For Geordie Fordyce I tried my hardest to obtain fitting
recognition of his heroism.

In any field of battle he would have unquestionably been
decorated; the Commissioner of Civil Defence concurred and put
forward his name but local confirmation was not forthcoming.

The reason? As voiced to me by a prominent townsman;
"Some people don't like Geordie Fordyce."

It was ever thus with the Lerwegian; the memory of some
peccadillo of a man's grandfather or some fancied slight by the
individual lives on whilst any good he may do is "oft interred with
his bones."

For a Lerwegian to receive bouquets from his contemporaries
he would well nigh need to surrender his life and George Fordyce
all but did that.

It has been said to me that this island trait stems from the
fact that courage on the seas is so much a commonplace there that no
Shetlander can enthuse about it.

Be that as it may I would retort that not all of Lerwick's
feuars and heritors have ever been on blue water.

Allan Laurenson, Honorary Treasurer to the Gilbert Bain
Memorial Trust and a most lovable sea-wise friend, was another
whose supreme self-sacrifice could well have received commendation.

Allan became commissioned in the R.N.V.R. for local duty and
lost his life in an effort to save others from the devastation by
an up-swept horned menace at the South End of Lerwick.

He bestrode the mine and attempted to bend a hawser around
it as it bumped on the sea-lapped littoral.

The whole of Lerwick rocked to the cataclysmic detonation;
no longer was anything of the familiar figures of Allan Laurenson
and the Gordon Setter which was his constant companion, to be
seen in the town.

His brother, fortunately, remained to carry on the Laurenson
merciful tradition, as Honorary Secretary of the local Royal National
Life-boat Institution for many years.

*   *   *   *   *

Apart from the shattered frames and bodies which Tingwall
Hospital tended it achieved greatness in another sphere for, with
the Free Church just across the road from it, a splendid incentive
for a certain form of occupational therapy for convalescent patients
was immediately available.

True, this occasioned, from my point of view, a severe casualty list amongst my prettiest nurses but as this was of a Hymeneal nature I couldn't really complain.

Up the aisle of that picturesque little country church I had, on repeated days, to give them my right arm, right up to the altar where would be awaiting a Free Norwegian, a British Marine-Commando, a New Zealand flying man or even some ensnared Canadian hero — not all at once, but just as they fell, one by one!

From time to time I still hear from these couples and, as far as I am informed, every match has been a success.

The Matron of Tingwall, Miss Jessica Henderson, who was to be personally thanked for her services by the General Officer Commanding in Chief, Scottish Command, was an eminently suitable person for the particular task of caring for these men, often engaged in operations of a highly secret and dangerous nature.

Her own male kin were involved in intrepid defiance of the enemy in the Baltic, running the gauntlet to bring over here essential munitions from Sweden, such as ball bearings, carried on specially built high-powered diesel-engined craft and even, in the case of an uncle master-mariner who escaped from Narvik, to bring to home waters a convoy of several merchant ships, right through the Skaggerak, a channel but eighty miles wide in parts.

Her discretion could thus be relied upon in a hospital prominent on the landscape but one which, by reason of the safety of some of those in it and their relations in Gestapo-ridden Norway, had to be shrouded in a mantle of secrecy.

It was a loss to Shetland when that county was deprived of Miss Henderson's services but Clackmannan is the gainer.

With me she rates with Sally T. as a Nurse.

CHAPTER XV

The epic of the Norwegian Naval Independent Unit has been told in part by my friend, David Howarth, second in command to Major L. H. Mitchell, Officer Commanding, in his "Shetland Bus," vividly poignant in the baldness of its narration.

Fishing boats, each having a genuine registration number but always for a different area than the one where actual operation was undertaken, were used for this Shetland-Norway traffic. The crews were Norwegian in British service, receiving civilian pay and bonus. They were a Naval Unit under the command of an Army officer, controlled by the Admiralty and taking orders from the British Intelligence next to Madame Tussaud's in London. To add to the general contrariety but for a totally unknown reason they called themselves Military Establishment No. 7. Colonel Wilson who controlled Special Operations is now Hon. President of the Boy Scout's International Bureau.

The missions for the boats were varied but in general were the carrying of agents, saboteurs, arms and other materials. One special enterprise was undertaken by the outstanding skipper of them all, Leif Larsen in his sturdy little *Arthur* against 40,000-ton colossus, *Tirpitz*.

A journey would frequently consist of a thousand miles, usually in appalling weather for the boats needed the months when there was darkness, they being under constant watch by the enemy.

Arrived in Norway their safeguards were faked cargoes, forged papers and superlative courage.

Originally, Leif Larsen, who had been a volunteer in the Finnish campaign, escaped in a small boat to Shetland, unconsciously following a secret route already in use by the British Government for maintaining contact with Norway.

He was initially interrogated by the British Intelligence Service in the Royal Victoria Patriotic School for young ladies in Battersea but ultimately earned more British decorations than any of our own nationals.

"Shetland's Larsen," C.G.M., D.S.O., D.S.C., D.S.M. (and bar) was first chosen for the select company bearing his own name by

Martin Linge, whose record was a by-word among Norwegians. He was unhappily killed in action later that year.

After training with the Linge Company at a manor near Oxford where he was introduced to the rather astonishing behind-the-scenes picture of Britain-at-war Leif was away up on the West Coast of Scotland where he learned the secret deadly techniques of killing and survival. He delved into the right and the wrong way to perform every kind of sabotage and a most efficient way, with economy of effort, to slaughter a man even if one's weapons were limited to the fingernails.

Next followed Birmingham for parachute jumping and also the school of espionage, near that city, for ciphering messages and general intelligence organisation.

Apart altogether from these multitudinous courses in the stately homes of England and Scotland the man himself is one whose whole life fitted him for his great task but there are no tricks in plain and simple faith such as is his.

He is a quiet and self-effacing person, of stocky build and has a lean face now attractively marred, to my way of thinking, by a broken nose!

It is said by authority, with regret I must admit, that Larsen was not given the Victoria Cross because he is a foreign national. His friends cannot understand this for the supreme award was given to Lars Lassen, a Dane, and like him, Larsen held a commission latterly in the Imperial Forces.

Leif, however, who now is in command of Norway's Maritime Home Guard, would never voice such a thought for if ever a man's life reflected this verse, it is his: "When I'm not thank'd at all, I'm thank'd enough; I've done my duty, I've done no more."

But Leif Andreas Larsen *did* do more — he gave something far transcending any human demand.

The saga of Tingwall Emergency Hospital, battered at times by nomadic Heinkels, in its unwelcomed proximity to a military encampment, remains to be unfolded, in all its documentary of not only Allied heroism but of our own courageous kind.

No written records are available to anyone as the nature of much of the work demanded suppression of even clinical notes and, with invasion an imminent peril, all diaries, maps and the like, were destroyed in fire by orders emanating from Lord Cork and the Deputy Commissioner of Civil Defence, Mr Bill Scarth.

But deeply engraved in the tablets of my own memory, in the nature of things the sole recollecting medium there can be of the entire picture, is a record of courage, audacity, fortitude and self-sacrifice on the part of those we were privileged to serve.

In all, I was favoured in Shetland to care for four recipients of the supreme award, the Victoria Cross, two of them made post-humously.

The surviving one I recall most vividly was Flying Officer J. A. Cruickshank. The official citation gave the number of wounds in that man's body but truth to tell that could be but a rough estimate.

*   *   *   *   *

Not only the fishing boats of the *Shetland Bus* came under enemy fire. The first trawler to be attacked, whilst engaged on its peaceful pursuit on the Shetland grounds was *Star of Scotland* with its Skipper Graham. This illegal case of murder was to initiate the guardian measures which the Royal Air Force undertook and promptly christened "The Kipper Patrol."

I went on board that ship when she came in. Never shall I forget the two oil-skinned six-foot figures lying prone on the deck, their hands, in death, still clutching the nets. The skipper, wounded and collapsed in the wheelhouse, had barely managed to make port.

Another hand lay dead in his bunk below decks. The machine gun bullets, unusually small and of hitherto unbelievable penetrative power, had gone through the iron-lined deck beams, as they had through the wheelhouse and even the tough smoke-stack.

At this time I was under secret orders to report to a special branch of Ordnance on any unconventional missiles or wounds I encountered in hospital practice. The search for phosphorous-coated projectiles was at its height.

Judge then of my dilemma when, on the day following my operation of bullet-extraction on Skipper Graham, a local general practitioner presented himself and announced that he wished to make an examination of my patient on behalf of the Ministry of Pensions. I had but newly been examining the three dead bodies under X-rays, a particular part of the duty imposed on me that I specially disliked, and I was now busy on my confidential report on these new penetrating missiles and the nature of the resultant wounds.

I fear I was a little curt in declining access to Skipper Graham.

The next thing, a week or so later, was a very worried gentleman on the telephone from Edinburgh. He spoke of some statutory right of examination for insured persons, the fee for which he mentioned as further proof.

I'm afraid I was equally abrupt with him.

There was another telephone message or two so the next time I was reporting to Ordnance I asked them if they would kindly take action to stop this absurd business.

Apparently this was done with expedition for I received a

long verbose letter from the Principal Medical Officer, Ministry of Pensions, in which he assured me everyone in his department appreciated my position.

Next time I paid my customary visit to the Department of Health, the C.M.O. tossed me over a file of lengthy correspondence, and from it I gathered I was a very bad boy indeed!

Anyway I was never troubled any more by Ministry of Pensions examinations of persons whose lives I was trying to save, insured or not insured.

*   *   *   *   *

With the North-Western Campaign nearing its climax at Narvik I was warned that Shetland might be called upon to provide a blood-bank service by air to Norway.

By the energetic help of Sir John Fraser, Chairman of the Scottish National Blood Transfusion Association, I had been able to form a cadet branch in our area and we also had a suitable storage refrigerator and abundant appartus for collection and donation. One of the general practitioners had made himself quite proficient with the type-testing sera.

The difficulty was in recruiting donors for, with the exception of a small core of faithful volunteers, the generality of people just would not come forward except to donate coin of the realm. This was welcome enough to a struggling Shetland Branch of the Association but it was a contribution that could not buy the very thing upon which the branch's own life depended.

We were never called upon to fly the blood over which was indeed a very fortunate matter.

However, with invasion so much in the air we decided that our lists must definitely be augmented.

Appealed to for his help Lord Cork's rather cunning ruse had a touch of Irish mischief in it.

He chose the very moment of egress from the churches on a Sabbath morning, and, at the head of his entire retinue of staff, black malacca cane, gilt-festooned cap and all, he marched right down the hill into the little hospital where, forthwith, he was the first to have his blood tested.

All this in full view of the town's best broadcloth and formal headgear.

The psychological effect was immense; it is even recorded that he inspired full employment of the jade, Mistress Rumour (one not entirely unknown within this island group!) and that it became the belief that, for those who were not so prepared the direful fate of evacuation from the area was impending.

Our donating lists soared and many a litre of good red blood, inspired by Ginger Boyle's own fine blue stuff, passed on its life-saving mission.

This weapon of rumour, recognised as a handy device by all Intelligence Services, was more than once put to good use in pursuance of some good cause.

It is an inalienable fact that some people have an cverweening compulsion to be "in the know."

"What's news wi' you?" is a common mode of greeting in the islands. This may be an invitation to disgorge any morsel such as your view on the prevailing price of a cran of herring or the juicier *entrecôte* of the present condition of Aunt Muti Jeannie's health with particular reference to the estimated net residue of her estate in the event of untimely demise.

All this is of great value for subsequent retailing "on the street."

On occasion the Puckish, poker-faced Highlander from, say, Argyll, arriving through the South Mouth and fully alive to this little foible, has been known to set in train an ingravescent tale of some particular moment to him by revealing exactly the opposite of what he wants to be known.

The game has many variations but with a little finesse the originator retains the initiative all along.

Thus, a disciple of physician Rabelais could appreciate the motives of Baron Boyle of Youghall when he intimated by pamphlet that the descent of hostile parachutists was to be heralded by the passing from ear to ear of the *single* code word, Blood Red.

To your knowing Lerwegian here was another typical Irishism; bumble-dom and bumble-dee now can number up to three, was chuckled around.

The alertness of Arcady, however, was a little too jejune to catch the twinkle in the eye of the former Naval Intelligence Officer when he made the gory signal.

Was it not preferable to have scorn and derision of a man big enough to take it, rather than fear and despondency, he well knowing he could fully rely on Shetland's grit if ever there was need?

There was a time, though, when I took delight in circumnavigating one of Lord Cork's little "bull" schemes.

A destroyer, *H.M.S. Zulu,* had fared badly, although victoriously, in a North Sea action.

The Number One became my patient through bomb splinters in the arm.

When the period of his convalescence after operation was completed I was walking down with him to the troop-ship on which he was scheduled to embark.

His winged arm was sling-borne and the empty jacket sleeve waved about rather untidily but he was the curly-headed, carefree, hatless type who gave no thought to his undoubted good looks.

Rounding a corner into the lane which would fetch us up at the harbour front we were horrified to come *vis-à-vis* Lord Cork.

"Where is your hat?" was fired at my charge.

"At the bottom of the North Sea, Sir;" my gallant Number One answered truthfully.

"Well, get it and don't attempt to appear again like that in public."

The malacca cane stumped off.

There is, I believe, known universally to the Navy an estimable Pandora's Box called Gieves but unfortunately this emporium has no branch in Lerwick. There was little doubt, too, that a signal would already be in composition for distribution to all concerned anent matters of correct dress for officers embarking.

Vigilance, thus alerted in the streets and at the gangway, would be impassable so improvisation must be invoked.

Whipping Number One into my room in the Grand Hotel I bandaged up his innocent head, being careful to display a good border of white below the khaki-coloured Balaclava from the Navy League's stores, with which I crowned him.

Thus, not only was Ginger Boyle, twelfth Earl of Cork and Orrery, Admiral of the Fleet, quite out-manoeuvred but *Zulu's* second in command, far from being barred, was piped aboard with all the solicitous care and attention his hero's hatless pate demanded.

Not all the Old Man's rulings were severe, however. One lady had cause to be grateful to him; after an interview with me at the hospital, in her own words; "It was only when I met thon Admiral I kent I had met a real gentleman."

To this wife of a patient I always thought Dorothy Berry's lines applied most aptly: "Whose noble praise deserved a quill pluck't from an angel's wing," and I am sure Lord Cork must have agreed if her address with him was the same as it was with me.

This all came about because her husband, whom I shall call Jim Hawkins, a fifty-year-old marine engineer from John Brown's Clydeside ship-yard had volunteered for active service.

After preliminary training at a seaside resort he had again volunteered for special service in which he was to control a powered assault craft.

It must be explained that even in those early days Britain possessed one or two of these vessels although not of the pattern with which we later became familiar as T.L.C.s or L.C.I.s.

Nor were commando formations yet in being although in the Narvik operations, certain independent companies were used to the south of the fjords with the mission of delaying the advance of the north-bound Wehrmacht.

But precisely what Jim Hawkins was doing driving a landing craft on to the coast of Norway, after Narvik, or how they got there, was certainly none of my business.

All I knew was that he was a very brave man and that the Germans thus early rumbled to the wisdom of liquidating the engineer on those boats, as all defenders were to learn later on, for so the assault troops or other parties on board instantly became more vulnerable.

In pursuance of this idea they shot him through the chest and he came to me with a hazardous injury, a sucking wound over one lung.

For such patients on the dangerously ill list I was empowered to summon the next of kin to the bedside; they came by air and were allowed to remain in the Protected Area for twenty-four hours.

When Madame made her entry into my office the green quill in her bonnet very nearly transfixed me between the eyes.

"Whit the hell's the meaning of this?" she demanded before I could even speak and her little bandy legs were literally trembling with indignation; "I was led to believe ma man was doon the water at the Lairgs learning young yins to be marine engineers. Whit the hell is he daein' away up here at the back o' beyont?"

Up and down went the green quill with venom in every dart it made before my wary eyes.

I explained as best I could that Jim was sorely wounded after doing something very brave.

Leaving her in the care of the Matron I tip-toed to the poor old man's side; "Jim," I said; "there's someone very important come to see you."

It did not take him long to guess whom I meant but brave and all as he had been in the face of the enemy he was anything but that now:

"Oh, my Gawd; No' the wife, is it?"

He strove to slide down his upright bed-rest to seek the haven of the sheets till I restrained him.

The Matron had been briefed to remove Mrs Hawkins instantly if there was one hint of disturbing sound from her.

As I was to be apprised, there was no occasion to worry; she sat by the bedside as quiet as a little mouse, just holding the hand of her stricken man.

Came the time when she must go home; I told her that the regulations stated her passage must be by sea. Demands on aircraft seats for essential travellers dictated this.

But Mistress Clydeside was having none of that; "I come here by an airyoplane and by an airyoplane I goes hame and, forbye, there's no' a yin o' you b——s goin' to stap me!"

"Very well, Mrs Hawkins; you'd better just go and tell the Admiral that."

I uttered this in a perfectly ironical way but she took me up at once:

"I'll dae that; whaur's he tae be found?"

She did find her way to the Bruce Hostel and saw the Admiral; his Flag-Lieutenant was ordered to arrange her air-transport and off she flew from Sumburgh aerodrome in an R.N.A.S. machine, the White Ensign fluttering from the nacelle in utter defiance of any menacing German aircraft.

Later I received her letter, quite illiterate but obviously the product of much painstaking labour. In it she made the reference to our gentlemanly Admiral and for my eye alone, she added quite contrary to what I expected; "God bless you."

In later life, his illustrious naval career concluded, Lord Cork continued to serve the cause of the men who follow the sea.

His speeches in the House of Lords have the one devoted inspiration, the sponsoring of improved conditions for the Merchant Navy.

It is in that connection, with particular reference to the one aspect of which I have some knowledge, Medical Aid by Radio, that I had the good fortune to re-animate an association, enhanced on my part by respect and affection.

The belief in a common cause was shared.

CHAPTER XVI

With the completion of a year's service in Shetland approaching I was giving constant thought to one other facet of a civilian surgeon's responsibilities, this towards a concern of vital moment to the islands' womanhood, the difficult labour.

The general practitioners, under the Highlands and Islands Medical Scheme were all, I say with respect, accomplished *accoucheurs* but they relied on surgical aid when the complicated case presented.

Now, it had worried me not a little at first to find that there was a bland acceptance that their surgeon should not only perform the operations of practically every known specialty but that he should do them with all the skill and expertise of the specialist in them.

He had to be the Pooh-Bah of the medical stage; abdominal surgery, thoracic work, tonsil removal, nasal deflections, radical mastoids, gynaecology, skin diseases, acute ophthalmology, expert X-ray interpretation and even a consulting physician's opinion were all expected from him.

Things have advanced since then but I was having to go it alone in these early days.

It did not appear to be within the compass of the people's knowledge that such combined versatility and virtuosity became a superman only and should the suggestion be made that a particular patient depart for the mainland in order to have treatment then one was apt to cause the whisper to go round; "The surgeon's baffled by my case and needs a professor to help him."

A very trifling prick, you may think, but it is an inevitable accompaniment to life in this island community that an intense interest is shared by all in health and its derangements, a morbid disposition, one might hold, of enjoying ill-health.

The Surgeon-Consultant stood alone in the splendid isolation of critical limelight and woe betide the reputation of the man who was unfortunate enough to have a fatality from such calamities as tetanus or a pulmonary embolus.

At first it caused me disquietitude but gradually I came to see that no real malice was intended; the matter was really just a heaven-sent focal point for a good gossip and such is the very breath of life in the North.

Curiously, I have not found this trait in other island communities, of Celtic or French derivation. The Lewisman, the Skyeman, the Manxman and also the Channel Islander all show reserve in these bodily affairs, even within their own intimate circle but reticence is not a feature of Scandinavian races; indeed the latter are in every way much more emotional than is generally thought and their quick sensitivity goes hand in glove with gossip-proneness.

Apart from any such considerations the responsibility of maternity work at first appalled me; the performance of a lower segment Caesarean Section was child's play to one versed in abdominal work but the problem was to decide when it was a justifiable interference and I flattered myself that my conscience was too sincere for me to adopt readily the easy escape from any difficult obstructed labour.

When I set foot in Shetland I had not even witnessed the birth of any living creature since I had done my midwifery course as a medical student in 1920 if we except the periodic and frequent gestations of our domestic puss, Lady Mary.

When, therefore, I was informed that a primiparous lady in a pre-eclamptic condition was coming in for termination of pregnancy there could but follow a feverish perusal of Johnstone's and of Eden's excellent manuals.

After partial absorption of the wiles of Mr Krause or the pros and cons of Mr Caesar I would begin to wonder what instrument a real obstetrician would use.

Then there would follow a devastating thought of all sorts of recondite haemorrhages and a huge catalogue of calamities.

Thoroughly confused by it all I would wisely, I think, decide to rely on my own native forefinger resources and leave the remainder to the best of all midwives, Old Mother Nature herself.

Sometimes though, in a sudden access of sheer inspirational therapeutics I would prescribe a good sixty grains of *Pulv.Jalap Co.* and, with the inevitable onrush of gathering optimism, came in time to regard myself as quite a one with forceps and patience.

The basic principles of my midwifery were not, however, culled from any textbook; they came from a pathologist of renown, Sir Robert Muir. He used to say to us students who were wont to stray away to Rotunda Maternity Hospital in Dublin or to Rottenrow in Glasgow; "Why waste six months' valuable time in studying how to meddle with what is, after all, a purely physiological process?"

Sir Bobby also inculcated into me a precept which, in the light of a Shetland experience in my callow days. I should have been better to ignore.

He was a top-level authority on all matters pertaining to the blood and, on the question of organic tests to decide if any woman was *en famille*, he one day patted John, his laboratory familiar, on the shoulder and told us; "Today's discourse, gentlemen, will be on the subject of the blood serum test for early pregnancy.

"A gentleman named Mr Abderhalden has obligingly provided us with the appropriate material and we have submitted the method to the most exhaustive trial in the laboratory.

"So far, we have conclusively proved that both John and myself are pregnant."

It would have saved me a reddening of the face if I had taken the precaution of having had something in the nature of Herr Abderhalden's authority when I opened the abdomen of a forty-year-old widow, relict of five years' standing, for the contemplated removal of a fibroid tumour and produced instead a pinky, nice little wiggley rabbit from the uterine hat!

The subsequent explanation for the duality of patients called for considerable tact when I came face to face with the anxious relations concernedly pessimistic about Auntie's being ever able to stand this big, internal operation.

The midwifery apart, I made early overtures for the assistance of specialists to be brought to Shetland. The earliest boon of this nature to be conferred upon the islands was in the ophthalmic sphere when the noted surgeon, Dr Beatrix B. Law, of the corresponding department in Aberdeen's Royal Infirmary, undertook to help of her own volition, her sense of social kindness being of so very high an order. Her chief of that time, Dr Harold Smith, to whose wards she was to succeed, already attended in respect of the Blind Persons Act, but Dr Law extended the whole range of services.

Professor R. S. Aitken, of the Department of Medicine in the same institution and subsequently Vice-Chancellor, first to Otago and then to Birmingham University, was also a tower of strength and encouragement.

I wanted him to arrange for a Resident Consulting Physician for the combined islands of Orkney and Shetland but I was ruled out on the grounds that it would be difficult to persuade a suitable man to reside there and it was doubtful if there was a sufficiency of work to justify the creation of such a post. A compromise was reached.

To this I still demur most strongly; for such a physician could also fulfil the dual office for which there is clamant need in the modern practice of medicine, of laboratory supervision and consulting practice.

The islands of Lewis and Harris, in the Outer Hebrides, have made a success of the appointment, with accruing benefit to the people.

In maternity work the occasional visit of an obstetrician was in a different category. Obviously he could not be on the spot when the sudden emergency presented itself unless by chance and so one was forced into self-reliance.

None the less his presence would have been welcome, if only to review the whole picture and advise on methods.

I was at one time reported to be resentful of visiting specialists but as the record shows the accusation was entirely a made-up one.

In these isolated areas a single-handed surgeon, bereft of any contact with his own kind, is forced to develop his own resources by extemporising in all directions. Lack of vision or unawareness of this, on the part of non-clinical administrators, obsessed with rules of procedure and a routine which blurs the fundamental reason for their own existence, the patient, is a very bad thing.

Administration is a vital concomitant for any hospital but it should be in the custody of those whose mentality is such that they can comprehend that a surgeon, concerned with human life, lives himself in feelings, in thought and not in figures on a dial.

Whilst undoubtedly I have met some very able administrators in the National Health Service, who understand the personal nature of good doctoring I have also met some of quite another kind.

In the hallowed atmosphere of the committee room which is, in theory, a chamber from which emanates the crystallised product of corporate opinion but can, in practice, emit the adopted view of but one or two dominant personalities, shrewd enough to disguise the fact, gossip can be euphemised into "public opinion."

According to the expediency of the moment decisions made can be "in deference to public opinion" and this can be a very potent factor in circumscribed areas.

Just as readily, on the other hand, the Pharisaical cry "in the face of public opinion," may be raised with telling effect in the nurturing of an air of courageous and self-immolating rectitude.

A specious presentation of facts need only then follow and the day is carried by the evangelist.

This is no sneering cynicism on my part; it is observed fact and is but one of the reasons why the adolescent National Health Service is a source of unrest with those whose primary concern is treatment of the sick.

In the old Voluntary Hospital system and in that of the Cottage Hospital, the Army Medical Services, the Highlands and Islands Medical Service and of the Colonial Medical Service every colleague I encountered was proud to belong thereto and said so.

Who ever heard of any medical man declaring his pride in

belonging to the British National Health Service as presently constituted?

Until an *esprit de corps* can be fostered in that service the ideals of its functions can never be accomplished.

But who will at any time enthuse over a system which could never undertake to meet the demands for urgent operations but for the Registrars and the Resident Surgical Officers who perform them, in the general usage of non-specialising hospitals, and yet these capable surgeons are denied the assurance of ever having any promotion?

I know personally one outstandingly good Registrar, highly qualified as M.B., M.R.C.P., who has unsuccessfully applied for one hundred and nine posts. He has been a Senior Registrar for seven years and has no guarantee that his employment will continue.

Considering that each lengthy individual application calls for twelve type-written copies, in many instances, is it to be wondered that accountancy looms largely on his horizon when the bill from the stenographer is presented to him?

True, he has been on the short list many times but this place of the élite is still just as good as a kick on the seat of the pants if not elected.

This moral wrong is no isolated case; I have travelled the country, north and south of the border, and what do I hear in every Residents' Mess I visit?

Cynical accounts of disillusionment, charges of nepotism and often distrust.

The medical profession itself does not prove to be a coherent body in these affairs; its sense of disquietitude is consequential to so many other bad features in the Service that only faint rumblings emanate from it. The one-time drastic step of proposed withdrawal from the Service by the general practitioners had its origins much more deeply placed than in mere £. s. d.

A sense of insecurity, based on lack of faith in the organisation, is prostituting a noble profession which is eager and willing to do its humanitarian duty if only it were properly inspired.

This end can surely be attained by a complete revolution in the organisation's approach to a profession which is, by the very nature of its calling, intensely individualistic. The change must be one to command the respect and the trust of the best elements within the ranks of ordinary practitioners, be they general or specialist, for they, after all, are the ultimate administrators of the Service to the People.

The alternative is to go on as at present and breed an entire race of doctors who, far from believing in ideals, will follow the pattern of pragmatism and view its horizons in the light of profit and loss accountancy.

Heaven knows we have enough of those already.

* * * * *

By the end of my first year in the North the broad plan for the future was taking shape if but ephemerally.

The kernel of the matter, as I saw it, was really based on something I had learned from my teacher Sir William Macewan, Lord Lister's assistant in Glasgow.

Sir Billy was an individualist. "We are in no sense a co-operator;" he was wont to say in his royal fashion.

That austere isolation may have been becoming in a pioneer of his stature but what was more applicable to a puny figure like mine was that he disdained the newer, hydraulically-operated type of table in his theatre.

"An able surgeon can perform equally good work on an ordinary wooden table;" was his pronouncement.

Without accepting this in a literal sense I considered that a newcomer to the islands, with a fresh outlook, should be able to exploit existing resources a little more and suggest other lines of development but, certainly, not all of a sudden.

By dint of constant representation we gradually accumulated an abundance of first class equipment.

Also, I have pleasure in recording, fine bodies like the Woman's Rural Institute, the "Ladies of Sandwick," the Shetland Branch of the Red Cross, of course, and others made helpful contributions in the way of theatre furnishings and other gifts.

At war's end, I may interpolate, the Army were sufficiently guileless as to leave a young subaltern in charge of all their hospital stores and he was persuaded that the proper application of the logistics of peace, was that a selection of this equipment should be diverted for safe, if only temporary, keeping to the civil hospitals.

These had come under a most bewildering classification, "Inclusion within the Emergency Hospital Service." What that had meant I never quite understood, save that I served, not one, but a heterogeneity of masters.

None the less this inclusion was a god-send for the subsequent bedevilment of assessors and inventory-makers who presented their compliments in person; the stores are there to this day.

H

CHAPTER XVII

The paper work in all these and other undertakings was overwhelming.

I had no typist; all correspondence had, of necessity, to be written out in my own fair hand and when it is recalled that the Forces alone, apart from the Ministry of Pensions, required the completion of innumerable forms, it is small wonder that I sat far into the night at my desk.

I had one part-time book-keeper who looked after the accounts but, like myself, he was bewildered at the start.

Even with his hard-working assistance, how ever we did manage remains a mystery to this day. My helper was Mr Peter Sutherland, later to be the able Secretary to the Board of Management, Shetland Hospital Group in the National Health Service.

I have before me Form 405 relating to an airman who, apparently, attended for something in the nature of a pimple on the nose.

There had been voluminous correspondence arising therefrom.

I was to "raise and complete" Forms MPC47 and, in addition, MP40 which "must bear a complete history of diagnosis, treatment including dietary and progress. All temperature charts, X-rays and reports of special examination must be enclosed."

In addition there is a postogram (at one shilling for thirty words!) from Wing - Commander, Officer in Charge, Medical Statistical Records, Ruislip.

The rubric of this gentleman's disquietitude is thus disclosed: "No. 694817, Warrant Officer Wisecrack was admitted to your hospital on 5.11.40. So far E.M.S. 103 has not been raised and completed by you for receipt in this office. This Form E.M.S. 103 must be completed and raised by you according to instructions issued to you and forwarded to the Local Casualty Bureau.

"If it is proposed to discharge any patient belonging to Royal Air Force personnel from your hospital you are to give me three clear days of notification so that instructions as to disposal and necessary railway warrant may be sent to you.

"Please see that all your staff are familiar with this procedure."

My first reply to this seems strangely polite if not couched in my best orderly-room phraseology.

(1) I have received no instructions.

(2) I do not possess Forms E.M.S.103.

(3) I do not know where the Local Casualty Bureau is nor does anyone else.

(4) I should be grateful to know to whom I should send my account for professional services.

The immediate reaction to this humble petition was forthcoming: "No. 694817, Warrant Officer Wisecrack was admitted to your hospital on 4-11-40. So far E.M.S.103 has not been received . . . " and so on as before.

The reply this evoked is in somewhat different vein but is an earnest of what I was enduring generally.

"I have the following observations to make and you will please take immediate and necessary action or refrain therefrom as the case may be.

(1) I am a civilian surgeon in the islands known as Shetland.

(2) These are surrounded by water and a Railway Warrant won't make the trains run.

(3) I am not a ruddy orderly-room clerk.

(4) I am not a sanguinary philanthropist.

(5) I am not prepared to subsidise the R.A.F. to the extent of purchasing envelopes big enough to hold your Forms M.P.C.47 nor the necessary postage stamps required by His Majesty's Postmaster-General.

(6) I am only too happy to oblige the Royal Air Force by offering surgical advice or treatment.

(7) A state of war obtains in Europe and these islands (incorrectly called the "Shetlands" by you) are so situated on the map, if you will but consult it, that for "three days" postal notice of dismissal you will read "three weeks" — that is if the patient hasn't gone home already.

(8) If any more such bumph is received from you it will go in the fire.

(9) I will do this myself as I have no staff.

(10) All the same we will win this war.

(11) Cheerioh to you.

I heard that the R.A.F. framed it and hung it up in the Mess at Ruislip. Anyway, it served the purpose and future demands were much more circumspect.

At this time, too, I was beginning to think in terms of an assistant. True, the Services, by now, had a few medical officers but, having their own station duties to perform, they could not give me the whole-time help I desired.

My most adjacent junior was a naval Surgeon Lieutenant, a

Hibernian named Donnan, hailing from a town, I thought most appropriately, called Hollywood. There, according to himself, for the period of his R.N.V.R. service, his locum was his father who was "lettin' the whole show go to hell."

He looked after the immediate requirements of the naval hospital, to which I was consulting surgeon, and I conceived the idea that if a naval junior consultant were appointed there we could work harmoniously together.

The Department of Health could not help as they had no one available. Later on they sent up a very competent and decorative lady who was of great help.

"Glamour M.D." the troops were to christen her, but that was with all respect.

My approach was then made to Surgeon Rear-Admiral Sir William Wheeler; already he was in constant touch with Maxwell-Scott, a particular friend of his, and the surgeon frequently helped me as courier in matters Shetlandic which I did not care to commit to the censored mail.

Sir Walter, in his turn, was in almost daily liaison, not only with St. Andrew's House but with Vice-Admiral Tovey, commanding Western Approaches at St. Enoch's Hotel, Glasgow.

Wheeler was entirely sympathetic to my representations but he interpreted them in his own understanding way and provided me thereby with the greatest personal problem which I had to face since agreeing to undertake the Shetland mission.

He wanted me, in the first place, to put up the proposal for the appointment of a civil Admiralty Agent, a surgeon from outwith the islands. To this I would not agree as it would have displaced the local general practitioner already acting in that capacity and I had no wish to do that.

I then received a confidential letter from a co-ordinating branch of the Central Medical War Committee.

In it reference was made to my post-Munich undertaking to serve anywhere with a preference expressed for the Royal Navy.

The communication continued; "On verbal advices received from Surgeon Vice-Admiral, Director-General of Naval Medical Services, we are empowered to offer to you employment as consulting surgeon in his department.

"You would be granted temporary rank in the Royal Navy commensurate with your duties and the emoluments would be stabilised at their present level in accordance with existing regulations laid down for the remuneration of civil surgeons serving with H.M. Forces durng the period of national emergency.

"The transfer would be effected by seconding from your existing Territorial Army Reserve commitment to the Royal Navy.

"We are further authorised to say that a continuation of your present interim duties, of which we have been apprised by the Permanent Secretary to the Department of Health for Scotland, who has been informed of this intention, is contemplated but with certain extensions thereof, contingent upon your being based on the Royal Naval Temporary Hospital, Kingseat, Aberdeenshire.

"We ourselves would add that it is understood by the Admiralty that the performance of your duties in your present interim capacity would be facilitated by this temporary appointment.

"It would be appreciated if you would regard this communication as confidential and urgent and forward your decision to this Committee at an early date in order that necessary action may be expedited by the departments concerned.

"We have the Honour to be, Sir, your Obedient Servants," etc., etc.

Here was a poser indeed!

At first consideration thus was the way opened wide to be freed from all the pin-pricks of pettifogging officialdom; freed from all the anomalous position of this Emergency Hospital "inclusion" whereby I received certain instructions in respect of the hospitals whilst the Trustees responsible for the administration under the Highlands and Islands scheme, knew nothing of them.

Gone for ever would be the arguments with brigadiers as to gas-proofing and the like, no more bickerings with stuffy little majors.

Furthermore, I would have a competent and adequate staff with a well-run office.

I would be freed to practise the art of surgery and look after my patients without any harassment from minor figures in the profession.

I would be able to select my own assistants, without doubt, and look after the people of Shetland as they deserved, without having to worry whose patient was whose and what doctor was to give the anaesthetic. I could organise the pathological laboratory for which I craved without interference. As an added inducement here was to be the *cachet* of belonging to a Service I had come to admire and respect, one in which the administrators, in their elasticity, were much more knowledgeable of self-reliance than were other quarters with which I had to deal.

There seemed no obstacle to immediate acceptance.

But there was and it existed solely within myself.

It concerned largely the visiting of the homes in the outlying islands and in the country, an aspect of the surgeon-consultant's work I had come to love and look upon as the greatest of the all-too-few amenities in the appointment with its twenty-four-hour service taken for granted.

There was neither croft, cottage nor mansion which I did not consider it a privilege to enter; I had learned to respect and delight in meeting the simple, hard-working souls with their absence of deceit and artificiality.

A seat in the ben-room or in the kitchen with its plain wood scrubbed to perfect cleanliness, the sturdy table with white wax-cloth covering and the various other evidences of careful house management were entrancing to me as I listened to these honest, Godly creatures tell of their interests and activities.

As I wrestled with the problem of this new naval enterprise I had ever before me the vision of those crofts, on the walls of which one would see two or three pictures, all, to me, evocative of the life therein.

Victoria, sedate and velvet-bosomed, would survey the scene from her place above the peat-stoked Victoress stove.

"Another Queen;" would murmur the guernsey-clad master of the house as my gaze would travel to the coloured reproduction of an old-fashioned steamship putting out to sea, arrogance in every tall-sparred line of her as she flaunted her ascendancy over the newly-supplanted sail, carried, as it were, merely from a custom of the past.

The third wall decoration could well be the likeness of an oil-tanker, funnel right aft and the long belly of her passing forward to the high forecastle.

"My eldest boy's boat;" would murmur my host with restrained dignity.

In the corner too, I would see his reading matter: Borrow's "The Bible in Spain," Edward Gibbon's "Decline and Fall of the Roman Empire," Kinglake's "Eothen," Pliny's "Natural History," "Tait's New Seamanship and Nautical Knowledge," a haphazard copy of the "Kreutzer Sonata" by Tolstoi, beside the fiddle in its case.

I did not seek to bring once more to the surface of the ocean the earthly paradise of Atlantis but here, with these folk, I did feel that I could add my mite to the wealth of endeavour directed towards the uplift of human happiness.

The people's orderly life was already disrupted enough by the enforced militarisation of their land; they understood that was necessitated by national security but would they not feel cheated of almost the last personal and intimate service in their midst, a surgeon who was at least beginning to understand the peculiar circumstances of their lives?

How would it affect them when, say, Peerie Peggy of Burra was going to have her bairn and the surgeon she wanted to reassure her, and her family, crossed the threshold of the croft, to doff a dazzling gold-braided cap and roll up a sleeve encircled with mesmerizing rings?

Would the spontaneity of faith in God's mechanism of birth not fade away completely in the presence of this evidence of the Devil's own war-preparedness?

Whatever was the answer this reflects the cause of my doubts and I decided to have the advice of one I not only respected but revered, Sir John Fraser, K.C.V.O., M.C., F.R.C.S.

I was in the habit of sending him my thyroid cases, in which he was expert and on which I operated only with lack of complete satisfaction to myself, in the absence of immediate laboratory facilities and the constant supervision of a consultant physician

Born in the little northern seaport town of Tain Sir John knew and understood the life of the land and the sea, from Muckle Flugga in the north, to the River Tweed, aye, and beyond it too.

Often had I sent to him a patient of quite humble origin and circumstance.

Knowing the difficulties confronting such a pilgrim in the way of irregular travel from Shetland and one possibly in complete ignorance of the mainland's ways the arrangement he demanded was that such a Shetland patient should come, not to any Royal Infirmary, but directly to his house in Moray Place.

Such was the man who, as Professor of Clinical Surgery in Edinburgh University, and later its Principal, commanded emoluments commensurate with a practice that ranged from John O'Groats to London and, on occasion, beyond the shores of Britain.

He held amongst his other major positions, the one of Consulting Surgeon to the Department of Health and helped me, an erstwhile pupil, on many other occasions to my great content.

I was now, however, to find that the necessary leave of absence in order to go and see him was not quite the matter of routine that I thought it was to be. The onus of not only finding a locum but of paying him, to the tune of twenty pounds a week out of my own pocket, was placed upon me.

There were at this time no Service operating surgeons in the islands although latterly the Army always did relieve me and I found that these colleagues were even more indignant than myself at this "holiday without pay" injustice and never would they take a penny piece although perfectly at liberty to do so by King's Regulations.

I could have gone sick and forced the hand of officialdom for as a result of my year's labours, hopping in and out of small craft, the inclemency of Shetland's weather and similar rigours, I was beginning to have the first of many troubles with old wounds. Errant and migrant little bits of bone were inclined to pop out playfully from holdings where they had no right of tenure whatsoever, udal or feudal, and, at times, when very fatigued, I had difficulty in persuading joints that should have been supple to straighten out at all. I was living with pain.

Eventually, on my own personal grape-vine I heard of one consulting orthopaedic surgeon, David Keir, who was awaiting to take up appointment at the then assembling emergency hospital, Stracathro, near Brechin.

He was willing to come up and have a look at me and when he had seen my dressings taken down made, for his part, and out of the goodness of his heart, no bones at all at relieving me himself.

CHAPTER XVIII

Sir John and Lady Fraser received me with their usual charm and homely grace. Naturally, in his official capacity, he was aware of my contemplated naval excursion; he now filled in many details for me.

It appeared that "all of us who are interested," to quote Sir John's words, "realise your immense difficulties in trying to harmonise the opposing interests of civilian administrators and Service Chiefs.

"It is obviously impossible for any man to go on sigle-handed, as you have been doing, carrying out major operations, along with all the trifling work that crops up, not to speak of all the clinical tests in the laboratory we know you have improvised.

"I'm quite sure you've loved the challenge of it, all the same, Dan."

I could not but agree with a nod of my head.

He went on; "You will not know it but your peace-time Shetland predecessor may not be too happy in the situation he finds himself in the Forces.

"If it were acceptable to him it could be suggested he be released and return to Shetland.

"For your part they'll likely give you flag rank and you'll be able to disperse the duties as you like, up to a point, but I don't think you'll see the crofters and the cotters any more; you and he would have to arrange your operating sessions between you but the civilian work would largely be his responsibility under the H. & I. Scheme which we mean to keep going as long as we can."

As I pondered over this enlightenment, Lady Fraser dispensed coffee and my Uncle Dan, Professor of Divinity, came in to join us.

Then Sir John said: "I would remind you, before ever you decide, that any rank, Surgeon Rear-Admiral, Air Vice-Marshal, or any other, can never take the place of sheer personality in our profession and, when it gains the day, counts for far more in the way of inward satisfaction."

When he said that I was reminded that he was the man who, but a brief time before, had rushed aboard the destroyer *Mohawk,* badly hit in Rosyth Basin when the Huns were attacking the Forth Bridge, sent all busybodies about their business and, there and then, transfused the wounded captain as he lay upon his wrecked bridge.

He was also the man who had stormed the citadel of official dilatoriness, in response to my *cri de coeur* for transfusion equipment during Norway's torture, and scattered the time wasters by his vehemence; "Get a refrigerator and a hundred sets from Professor Cappell's blood bank flown up to Lamont from Leuchars this very day!"

John Fraser, the fighter, had not been given the Military Cross for doing nothing!

In the charming drawing room at 20 Moray Place, Lady Fraser, in that gently smiling way of hers, had interposed; "Don't you give up what you're doing, Mr Lamont; I know John doesn't want you to."

Then the Right Rev. Professor Daniel Lamont, D.D., spoke and his words must carry weight.

In his "The Anchorage of Life," although he was both a mathematician and theologian of world renown his bias as the former is shown by his tending specially to that borderland between religion and science; thrown into relief is the superlative quality of his hold upon revealed truth.

I know this and I know too that vast academic honours and decorations sat lightly on my uncle's shoulders; not a mention of such had he ever seen fit to permit in "Who's Who."

But I also remembered that he was the man for whom his students showed their enthusiasm in an unprecedented demonstration. After getting him into a carriage they drew him through the streets of Edinburgh to the Old Quadrangle of the University, via the Bridges and Princes Street from New College on the Mound. He was then carried shoulder-high to the doorway where he was met by the Principal; all this was accompanied by ringing cheers and the singing of "Danny Boy."

Now he spoke to me quite briefly; "The giver of the greatest Service ever presented to humanity, Dan, was once clothed in the work-a-day dress of a carpenter."

That decided me.

This time I went back by *S.S. Highlander,* later to be sunk by torpedo, presumably as reprisal for her staunch feat of shooting down on this run two Heinkels, one of which she carried into port, proudly stacked upon her poop.

Muirhead Bone was to make an etching depicting this *tour de force* and it was carried in the "Illustrated London News," a broadcast of publicity not altogether appreciated by either her crew or other Shetlanders!

On my voyage on her back to the increasing stridency of War, little did I think, gazing aloft at the Golden Yardarm in my most prophetic moments, where the broad, turbulent, mine-ridden sea-lane was leading me — into the face of even greater stark horror; dismembered remains hurtling in the torpedo's wake, from out of the clouds and up from the ocean deeps.

But it led me too into the hearts of many kind souls and into the arms of one who was to be my companion for life.

Havoc, shells, bombs, bullets — love, bravery untold and laughter too.

Cunning, intrigue, avarice — sorrow, loyalty, self-sacrifice and joy.

Contrasts in life; Life itself a contrast.

*   *   *   *   *

When I wrote to Sir John Fraser to tell him I was back as before and had been given a young South African F.R.C.S., Surgeon-Lieutenant Domassie as my own assistant he replied with native generosity; "I am sure your decision is the right one; all of us in the Department of Health have reason to know that it will be received by the islanders with deep satisfaction."

Whether or no that was indeed a true forecast I shall never ascertain.

From one quarter, however, there was awaiting me an uproarious welcome and of gladness occasioned by my return, there could be no doubt here.

This was my little dog, Winston, who, in this extensive scene of crowds without company, as it was for me, was my sole confidant at that time. The two professional colleagues with whom I had really most in common were distantly situated, one at Levenwick in the south and one at Voe, where I loved to worship of a Sunday morning in the little church by the shore and join in the lusty singing

In this fjord-placed hamlet George Hendry lived, a puckish, shrewd little doctor of the old school. In bygone days, before the advent of the Highlands and Islands Medical Scheme, he would pay his visits on a pony, his lancets and nostrums carried in a ditty-bag culled from some sailor-patient and slung from the saddle.

For this item of service to a sick person, needing twelve-hour travel, he would charge a fee of four and sixpence, including his mount's fodder.

In later days the pony burgeoned into modernity in the form of a motor car for the hire of which he paid three guineas.

His fee remained at four and six.

To come back to little Winston; his lineage could lay small claim to impeccability, poor dog, but in other ways he did indeed possess some of the qualities of the House of Marlborough.

The soft brown eyes, exuding adulation, were framed within a fuzzy-wuzzy little mask of black and white. The whole revealed his loyalty and tenacity, confirmed by the grim velvet of his muzzle, no doubt donated by a mixed parentage in which some unspecified terrier breeds were conjoined. The slender brownish legs belonged somewhere outwith the reach of definition but they could well carry him to perform a dance of doggy gaiety, no less than to chase innumerable motor cars.

Quite clearly some Shetland collie charmer had been the object of amorous advances but then, what of it? Does the patriot, on Trafalgar Day, haul down the flag for shame of Lady Hamilton? Does the most rigid psalmist halt his singing on the thought of Uriah the Hittite, murdered for the lust of the author-king?

Winston's intelligence too rated high, clearly more than eleven-plus!

When one of these motors, quite justifiably, ran over his body, he betook himself off down the hill, in full cry, entered the Gilbert Bain and took up position at a certain door, tongue pantingly protruded and injured ribs supported in approved, first aid-begging posture.

He was outside the X-ray department!

Quite reprehensibly, his nocturnal resting place, the eiderdown at the foot of my bed, was the scene of many a frolic in which we both took part.

Of me, at no time, could I say, with the essayist, that I was never less alone than when by myself and I was soon to become a casualty; an occurrence which at first provoked my Winston to deep indignation but later gave him nought but a shared devotion.

I was shot through the heart — by an arrow discharged by that other marksman, Dan Cupid.

My life's partner to be happened to be the grand-niece of Arthur Anderson, M.P., founder and chairman of the Peninsular and Oriental Steam Navigation Company. This local Lerwick boy became a great national and Islands benefactor — just another example of Shetland's gifted sons.

Now, I was to have two patient listeners who would give polite attention to the expounding of my philosophy on the riddle of life, the one to answer, "Yes, dear, will you watch the potatoes?" and the other to wag: "Quite so, Master; now let's all go for a jolly walk."

Truly, but yesterday the word of Caesar might have stood against the world!

Nowadays, my friends all say that I stayed away from the teaching centres for too long. "The sheep in Shetland were beginning to treat you as one of their own," they say.

At war's end, anyway, when, in weariness of body and of mind, the thought of even the beloved Royal Infirmary and the treadmill of the Nursing Home system presented anew, the call of the pale, unripened beauties of the North prevailed.

The Department offered me the appointment on a permanent basis and the Gilbert Bain Memorial Trustees acquiescing, I then resigned from all my Glasgow hospital posts.

Certainly, by this action, the great financial rewards of consulting practice were abandoned; compared with the part-time hospital sessions of the National Health Service in prosperous England, the whole-time work in Shetland, where private beds are unknown, was, to quote the phrase employed in the Report of the Dewar Commission which initiated the Highlands and Islands Medical Service, almost entirely "eleemosynary."

But then, what of it? I congratulate myself that, for my equipment, in place of a heart there never was substituted any cash-register nor was self-commiseration a thing I ever liked.

On the contra side of the account there is the knowledge of well-intentioned effort and if only I have earned, in ever so small a measure, the remembrance by occasional mention in the prayers of the Far North, I am well repaid.

What I do know, moreover, is that I gained the awareness of approbation from Sir John Fraser and by that I mean too that I have won the knowledge of the greatest asset to be possessed by any surgeon.

It is recorded on the memorial tablet in the place of his birth.

When, on a certain day of remembrance, I last made my pilgrimage to the Parish Church of the little seaport town near Dornoch Firth, I found one other kneeling there before the window of stained glass.

Without the need for any word spoken John Fraser's one-time theatre nurse and I gazed together on the polychrome within that ecclesiastical embrasure.

Silently, within our hearts, we could but agree that the artist had limned well the very soul of his fellow craftsman.

The Figure of the Christ, a child borne in His arms, is accompanied by but the simple and the shining words, In Pity.

APPENDIX

The defection of the initial and errant Matron on my arrival in Shetland and her obvious disapprobation of the existing hospital arrangements were certainly instrumental to some extent in strengthening my resolve to propose directions for improvement. Immediate requirements were embodied in my *cri de coeur* to the Department of Health that the sole defence against air attack of the building was the "Pious hope that it won't be hit!" The result of that was extensive re-inforcing with beams and protective sand-bagging.

The next requirement was a Resuscitation apartment and this took the form of a concrete erection, duly fitted with piped oxygen, thermostatically controlled heating system and hand-operated ventilators of louvre pattern. This ward proved invaluable in the immediate care of ship-wrecked survivors of varied nationalities — Norwegian, Arab, Greek, Finnish, Swedish, British and Icelandic. At one time, before Norway and Denmark were over-run torpedoing of neutral shipping was of almost nightly occurrence.

Then there had obviously to be additional hospital building, of however temporary a nature. When Admiral Lord Cork evicted us from the Bruce Hostel the compliance of the Church of Scotland Trustees, in letting us occupy and build hutments around Tingwall House was greatly fortified by my Uncle Dan's intercession; he happened at the time to be Chairman of the Finance Committee of these same Trustees!

All in all I think our war-time arrangements worked very well. True, also, to my own disposition towards probing and pioneering I took it upon myself to submit to the Department, via the Hospital Trustees, a succession of papers headed "Improved Medical Services in Shetland."

Latter day developments saw the outcome of these proposals, in most, if not in all instances.

There was the inauguration of a Physiotherapy Unit, which was housed in a hutment transferred from Tingwall Hospital. The funds for the erection work and the equipment of the unit were canvassed by myself. This came about by my association in Glasgow with a well known surgeon, Mr J. Russell, who happened to be

Chairman of a Scottish offshoot of the Nuffield Trust — a Crippled Children's Association. I asked for one thousand pounds at a personal confrontation. Mr Russell shook his head — and my heart sank. "You will require fourteen hundred pounds!" was his cheering ultimatum. Later we were fortunate in securing the services of a very charming lady physiotherapist, Mrs Pat Frazer.

Maternity bed accommodation was another clamant need: the former Wrens' quarters, Nisson huts in Lover's Loan, were converted into a maternity annexe. No great imagination is needed to perceive the full play given to the wags of Lerwick who were greatly inspired by the address and the former gallant inhabitants!

No modern surgeon would attempt major work without the availability of laboratory assistance. The prevailing system was to send material by post to the City Hospital, Aberdeen — obviously a time-consuming exercise, apart from the likelihood of deterioration of the specimens in transit. The solution here was another cannibalised hut from Tingwall — brought over in its entirety so that sub-divisions could be placed as further needs might arise. Professor Aitken in Aberdeen undertook to give some initial training in his department, in blood counts and other measures. A former patient from Tingwall and a young man who had some experience as a chemist was chosen — Graham Robertson; Bacteriology, albeit inexpertly, was done by myself.

One fundamental requirement, that of a splint and appliance maker was filled by Mr Alec Leask. He attended a course in the subject at Stracathro Hospital, near Brechin. His great artistry had to be seen to be appreciated — splints of all kinds, footwear and even violins!

At Stracathro Hospital also I investigated and laid the foundations to make available to Shetland a project so very dear to my heart — the establishment of a Rehabilitation Centre as Shetland's War Memorial. Although pamphlets were written and distributed I doubt if my propaganda work was entirely adequate. The idea seemed to get about that "Rehabilitation" was synonymous with "Physiotherapy." Of course, this was not so. The training in an appropriate centre — Industrial or Hospital — of the disabled for alternative employment was the corner stone of the whole system. My target for this training for Shetland's disabled was to have been the heavy engineering workshop of Stracathro. (This was presided over in those days by a jaunty, muscular, trousered lady of most becoming appearance!) Also, less exacting training was to be available at a Red Cross estate on Loch Lomond-side. The Ministry of Labour were willing to help at Cardonald, near Glasgow, with their Industrial Rehabilitation Centre.

I had thought that such a restorative establishment for injured people would have been a wonderful and fitting memorial to those of Shetland who did not die in vain.

However, the plan seemed to diminish. A Hall of Remembrance in the New Gilbert Bain Hospital was, I believe, the remnants of the more elaborate project.

I have noted recently, an account of the up-to-date Health Centre. Certainly this is much more majestic than was my modest proposal — modest, yes, but a Health Centre indeed submitted in plan. I wanted a rota of doctors to visit suitably adapted premises in a disused hangar located in the fishmarket. There, minor injuries and sudden emergencies would be initially seen, thus saving the afflicted a tiring journey up hill to the hospital. The pressures on that hard pressed institution would lessen.

I had also put forward the idea that therein would be accommodated Mr Pete Shewan, who was the Resettlement Officer and who was to have been an integral operative in my Rehabilitation Unit. I had already worked most harmoniously with him.

A second but temporary thwarting of a personal project occurred in the use of B.C.G. vaccination for the protection of Shetland's children against Tuberculosis.

When I was the guest of the Norwegian Government on King Haakon's birthday in July, 1945, I learned that the Norwegian medical men knew nothing of Penicillin. By invitation I addressed the faculty on this subject, the discovery of Sir Alexander Fleming. The Germans had censored out all reference to the antibiotic in "Acta Scandinavina," the equivalent of our British Medical Journal. The Norwegian doctors declined to read it. They concentrated their activities on a compelling internal problem, Tuberculosis. My friend, Dr Johan Heimbeck, was a leading protagonist in this campaign and he, along with others, initiated me into all the complexities of the vaccine known colloquially as B.C.G. Dr Heimbeck was willing to supply the material if I could obtain an import licence from my own people. (I subsequently learned in a visit to Dublin, from a Dr Vera Bruce, all about obtaining such a licence, and how she organised her B.C.G. sessions). I thought that a comparatively closed community such as the Shetland Islands would be ideal for skin testing and vaccination. It was however too much in advance of the times and the plan was rejected, later, in a matter of years, to be adopted. However, my reports on the matter were received with profound interest by the Epidemiologist of the Department of Health who told me that I had brought the first description of the tuberculosis-combating techniques to Scotland. Resultant on this, the late Professor Sir James Learmonth of Edinburgh, and an experienced bacteriologist were commissioned to investigate further and off they went to Norway to bring back much more sophisticated data than was within my competence.

Reference to my Norwegian visit recalls to my mind that I escorted a fleet of ambulances, the gift of the Scottish Branch, British Red Cross Society, to the corresponding Norwegian body. That was pleasurable, but not so was a task assigned to me by the Imperial War Graves Commission. I was conveyed to a common and open grave wherein rested the bodies of executed Norwegian patriots, each one with occipital bullet wounds. My assignment was to examine all limbs, to confirm the presence of fractures, sustained prior to death, as a result of torture by Gestapo operatives.

In every case such was found by me.

In their subjugation under Nazi rule the hospitals suffered severe deprivation of everyday surgical materials, bandages, lint, catgut and other essentials. I compiled a list of these and in due course the Scottish Branch, Red Cross, sent supplies. I still treasure many charming letters from grateful recipients.

In conclusion, let me recount the story of Lieut. Dan Ravn, and his sister Fru Husabye, whom I met in Oslo, and subsequently was happy to have as a guest in Lerwick. I think the account typifies the spirit of Shetland.

The young Norwegian Naval Officer was a flyer, under surveillance by the occupying forces. In spite of this he succeeded in purloining a Heinkel and what was even more remarkable he refuelled it. In his black cross-marked machine he took off for Shetland: he knew no recognition signal of the day and the inevitable happened. British arms shot him down; his body came ashore at Gulberwick. My duties involved a post mortem examination and I could but confirm the origin of the lethal missiles. He was buried in the little area on the Knab reserved for Norwegian Nationals.

When I visited Johan Heimbeck in the Røde Kors Klinikk he presented me to Fru Husabye, who was there to meet me. I learned then that she was a leader of the women's section of the Home Front, and she, a farmer's daughter, had dwelt throughout the occupation, in the lodge gates of the Crown Prince's summer residence outside Oslo. The remarkable feature of that was that Vidkun Quisling occupied that main house, with shuttered windows and spy holes. Fru Husabye had kept the disloyal major under constant supervision and was never incarcerated, although questioned, as was Dan's wife. These women divulged nothing.

At my meeting with her I gave her what I had brought with me, excellent Lerwick photographs of "Shetland Times" artistry, of her brother's grave, on the little Knab reservation. Her intention then was to come to Lerwick and arrange for Dan Ravn's disinterment

I

and reburial in his beloved Norway. In due course I escorted her to the grave-side. No word of this visit had been voiced to anyone; what met the bereaved sister's eyes were beautifully tended and be-flowered Norwegian resting places. A supreme adornment was the little, beloved Norwegian flag on each tomb. Responsible for the loving care were voluntary ladies of Lerwick, whose names were not available.

Fru Husabye made no delay in her decision, "Dan will remain here. He lies with his face to Norway. Shetland cares;" and so it was.

*   *   *   *   *

Looking back to the days of the Dewar Commission on medical care in the remote Highlands and Islands, when, even in 1922, it records that treatments in the Highlands could be by incantation, I see the apotheosis of progress in the New Gilbert Bain Hospital, opened by Her Majesty the Queen Mother in 1961.

Seated just below the rostrum, from which Her Majesty spoke, I could not restrain the rising of a lump in my throat at these words: "The people of Shetland, the members of our Armed Forces, seamen of many nations and voyagers on the 'Shetland Bus' — all had reason to be grateful for the heroic way in which the doctors and staff of the old hospital refused to be deterred by the problems that faced them."

Leading to the culmination of a new order of hospital affairs in Lerwick I see too the roll of the dedicated men, each of whom added his quota to this march of progress: Rose Innes, Robb, Sturrock, Dick, Anderson. They all gave something lasting; and no beneficent state aid was there to make things easier for them.

There is no doubt in my mind that the present regime will ornament its heritage of healing and high tradition still further.

Fru Husabye's words remain true, Shetland cares.

THE END